1961

$25-12

THE SATURDAY BOOK

TWENTY-FIRST YEAR

THE SATURDAY BOOK

21

EDITED BY JOHN HADFIELD

PUBLISHED BY HUTCHINSON OF LONDON

THE SATURDAY BOOK

was founded in 1941 by Leonard Russell and has been edited since 1952 by John Hadfield. This twenty-first annual issue was made and printed in Great Britain at Tiptree, Essex, by The Anchor Press, Ltd, and was bound by Taylor, Garnett Evans & Company Ltd at Watford in Hertfordshire

The still-life painting on the title-page is by Joris van Son (1623–1667) and is reproduced by courtesy of Messrs B. Cohen & Sons, of Bury Street, St James's.

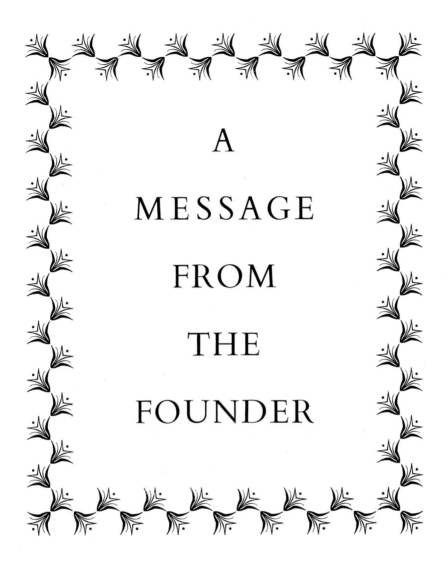

A MESSAGE FROM THE FOUNDER

JOHN HADFIELD tells me that with this issue *The Saturday Book* celebrates its twenty-first anniversary. Unbelievable! It seems quite a hundred and fifty years ago since I went to the publishers to propose a new annual miscellany, and they obligingly gave me a free hand with both the contents of the book and its physical appearance. Without this franchise, as you will see, *The Saturday Book* would have died in its infancy; for Number One was a Grave Mistake.

It appeared in the autumn of 1941, just when we were all becoming conscious that we were in (as Churchill said on the wireless at the time)

for a norful and norrible war: a stout, sparsely illustrated volume of essays and reminiscence. It was set upon by the reviewers, quite rightly, as an anachronism. This, they said, was no time for nostalgic memories of cricket, the English countryside, and all that jazz; and the pre-war paper on which the book was printed caused some hard feelings. One reviewer, bringing new standards to literary criticism, actually weighed the book on his kitchen scales, as if it were a chicken, and pronounced it, on the score of its Falstaffian bulk and big assemblance, a bad and unpatriotic book.

Something had to be done if the thing was to survive. Accordingly, I transformed myself overnight, editorially speaking, from a nostalgic into its opposite, a neoteric. Thus it was that Number Two was filled with the sound of martial music—or, at any rate, 'Colonel Bogey'. Apart from the pictures, which were numerous and tolerable, it all looked pretty terrible to me, and I was prepared to kiss *The Saturday Book* goodbye.

Strangely, it went down very well; and I soon perceived that it was the pictures that had saved the day. From there it was but a short step to conceive of the book as a richly illustrated super-magazine, produced with a care and craftsmanship which no magazine could rival.

And here it was that the publishers proved so generous. They let me incur enormous block-making expenses. They gave me adequate supplies of precious art paper. They allowed me to deal direct with printers, photo-engravers, paper-makers, binders. They even let me deliver review copies myself, and I seem to remember, on one occasion, dodging about Fleet Street and its neighbourhood in a taxi in the middle of a blitz. It was a great moment for both parties when John Betjeman called the book the best magazine in the world.

Thereafter, luck was on my side. I recruited Laurence Scarfe to design the book. I discovered two geniuses, Edwin Smith and Olive Cook, and prevailed upon them to supply, as they do to this day, a stream of extraordinary contributions. And when I found my work on the *Sunday Times* growing so demanding that I had to give up the editorship I had the best idea of all—John Hadfield.

John Hadfield has edited *The Saturday Book* for ten years now, evolving his own style, transforming the original formula into something different and better. Every year one marvels at his brilliance and resource.

Which leads me to the ironical conclusion that the best thing I ever did for *The Saturday Book* was to leave it.

LEONARD RUSSELL

THE FOUNDER. *Drawn by* H. ANDREW FREETH, A.R.A.

INTRODUCTION

TOP HAT, white tie, and tails—that is what the occasion calls for—not a curtain lecture on the influence of *The Saturday Book* upon popular culture. Over the years we have resisted the temptation to reveal the S.B. formula, to define its Aims and Objects. And we are not going to start now. When you reach the 'Retrospection' at the end of the book you can browse, if you wish, amongst some editorial *marginalia*. In the meantime—if you can take your eyes off Ginger Rogers and Fred Astaire—permit us to salute a few friends.

First, we make our salutations to Olive Cook and Edwin Smith, who, more than anyone else, are responsible for the Saturday Look. And we are particularly glad to have with them in this issue Laurence Scarfe, who designed the lay-out of the book before we ourselves took over the scissors and paste-pot. Then we want to salute our Constant Contributor, Fred Bason (sadly bereaved, since our last issue, by the death of that grand character, his landlady Liz). Fred is the cockney sparrow who makes so Saturdiurnal a contrast to our macaws and humming-birds.

Finally, we wish to salute The Founder, not only for inventing *The Saturday Book* but also for nominating ourself as his editorial successor. We used to wonder why, precisely, Leonard bowed himself into the wings. Now we know. The man who had given a new meaning to the word 'Saturday' felt, deep-down, the call to do something about the British Sunday. Which, as a Sunday journalist, he has brilliantly done.

. . . We will detain you no longer.   J.H.

BURLESQUE. *Painting by Michael Francis (Grabowski Gallery)*

[10]

CONTENTS

THE LOOKING GLASS OF TASTE AND FASHION

THE CABINET OF CURIOSITIES

WHEN I WAS TWENTY-ONE

ACKNOWLEDGMENTS TO PHOTOGRAPHERS

Associated Newspapers, p. 10; Associated Press, p. 28 (bottom), p. 31 (bottom), p. 41 (bottom), p. 48; B.B.C.: p. 25; Larry Burrows: p. 29 (top), p. 32, pp. 36–37, p. 41 (top), pp. 44–45; City of London Police: p. 16; Fox Photos: p. 19 (top), p. 27 (bottom), p. 28 (top), p. 34 (left); Tom Hustler: p. 47 (top); Keystone: p. 40 (middle), p. 43 (bottom); Donald McCullin: p. 43 (top), p. 46; Magnum: p. 40 (top); Mount Everest Foundation: p. 31 (top); P.A. Reuter: p. 47 (bottom l. & r.); Radio Times Hulton Picture Library: pp. 17, 18, 19 (bottom), 20–24, 25 (top), 26, 27 (top l. & r.), 29 (bottom), 30, 33, 34 (right), 35, 38 (left), 40 (bottom); John Sadovy: p. 39.

ALL OUR SATURDAYS

A Picture History
of Our Own Times

Compiled by
MONA PARRISH
AND THE EDITOR

1940

The Saturday Book was born into a crumbling world. It was conceived amongst such ruins as those depicted by John Piper at St Mary le Port, Bristol (*Tate Gallery*). It was compiled and edited despite such Fleet Street hazards as those illustrated above by Leonard Rosoman.

1941

Actuality
and apprehension

Whilst London fell in flames—
the building shown on the left
crashed into Queen Victoria
Street on 10 May—people still
waited in apprehension for the
terror that never came: gas. The
fantastic masks illustrated below
were designed for old people
and those with chest ailments.

[17]

1942

Women at war

A weeping girl waves goodbye as a troop train leaves Paddington station; Evelyn Laye, in a revival of *The Belle of New York*, keeps up the spirits of those who remain behind. Meanwhile, women recruited for war work wheel children in procession, demanding day nurseries.

1942

An interest in food

The thousandth Pig Club in Great Britain is formed—the Royal Household Pig Club. These pigs lived entirely on waste matter from the kitchens at Windsor Castle.

The new Archbishop of Canterbury, William Temple, fulfils his first public engagement—at a restaurant of the London Meal Service (1s. 6d. lunch of lentil soup, roast beef, two veg., plum tart, and tea).

1943 Coventry carries on

As the Rt Rev. Neville Vincent Gordon is enthroned as Lord Bishop of Coventry in February the Bishop's procession makes its way from the altar down the open-air aisle of the blitzed cathedral.

1944 Salute to an ally

To celebrate the achievements of our Russian ally, tribute is paid by Britain's war leaders at a gathering in the Albert Hall, where Sir Malcolm Sargent conducts the Royal Choral Society in a Salute to the Fighting Forces of the Soviet.

1944 One invasion has failed : another begins

The Nazi invasion has failed: another army—American—occupies Britain. 'Go, muster men!' says Laurence Olivier in the part of Richard III, as General Bradley attends a meeting of Army chiefs in London.

1945

The last throw

One last convulsive kick from the enemy before the war ends. One of the last V.2 rockets falls on Farringdon Market on 8 March, killing 380 people. Father Baines, parish priest from St Ethelreda's, Holborn, walks among the ruins. But the time has come for many Americans to bid farewell to their hosts, and Norman van Horne, of Saco, Maine, says goodbye to his English 'mum', Mrs Peacock, after being stationed for two-and-a-half years in an East Anglian village.

1946 Return to peace [24]

1947
New World
New Look

'Mr. Handley, *behave* yourself!'

Peace—it's wonderful! There's Her-
mione Gingold, at her *Sweetest and
Lowest*, singing 'I've had my portrait
painted by Picasso'. And there's Sheila
Sim, wearing the 'new look'.

1948 Debris of War

A 'displaced person' is deloused at a UNICEF centre.

Joy Nichols in *Take It From Here*   Harold Macmillan at The Hague

1948–50 New voices : new fashions

Gorgeous Gussie Moran takes the court at Wimbledon in lace panties.

1950
Top news:
Brumas

At the London Zoo the famous baby polar bear, Brumas, is born, and draws record crowds.

[28]

New slant
on an old sport

Eileen Fenton, 21-year-old 8-stone English schoolteacher, wins the £1,000 first prize for women in the cross-Channel race. She crawls the last few yards through shallow water on to Dover beach. Her time: 16 hours, 31 minutes.

1951

Top news:

Bevan

Nye Bevan, the rebel of the Labour Party, resigns from the Front Bench. Labour loses the Election.

[29]

New variations
on an old theme

Victor Pasmore at work on one of the huge murals for the South Bank Exhibition, hub of the Festival of Britain, organized to commemorate the centenary of the famous Great Exhibition of 1851 and to demonstrate the economic vitality of the country.

1952 Long live the Queen!

Queen Elizabeth II comes down the steps of the aircraft which brought her back from Africa on the news of the death of her father, King George VI. At the foot of the steps to meet her are Churchill, Attlee, Eden, Woolton.

1952—3

First man to climb the peak

Tensing, first man on the summit of Mount Everest, is photographed there by Hillary, 1953.

Last man to leave the ship

Captain Carlsen, captain of the *Flying Enterprise*, clings to the rails of his ship and refuses to abandon her as she lies adrift off the Cornish coast, 1952.

[31]

1953 Coronation Eve in Piccadilly Circus

Sentiment

Johnnie Ray at the Palladium

Sarcasm

Gilbert Harding at a TV party

Fervour

Billy Graham at Harringay Arena

Despair

Dorothy Tutin in *The Living Room*

1953–4 Expressions of emotion

1953 Dancing feet

Stanley Matthews gained his Cup-winner's medal when Blackpool won the F.A. Challenge Cup for the first time in their history.

One of the girls from Madame Dubonnet's finishing school near Nice—in Sandy Wilson's pastiche of the 'twenties, *The Boy Friend*, at the Players' Theatre.

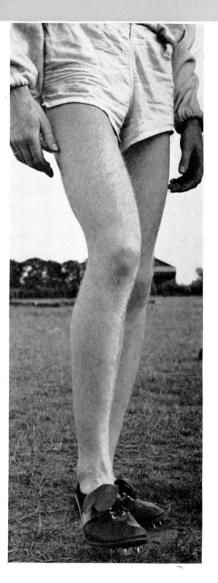

1954 Popular legs

The famous legs that ran a mile inside four minutes—Roger Bannister's.

The new-style 'Edwardian' trousers that branded the newly arrived Teddy Boy.

1955 Greatness sheds a tear

In the same week that he was given the Williamsburg Award Sir
Winston made his first major political speech since his retirement
at a Conservative rally in Woodford, his own constituency.
As the audience cheered, the old campaigner shed a tear. Then,
his handkerchief put away, Churchill chuckled.

1956
In Hungary:
Uprising

In Britain:
Liberace

In England the news-story was the arrival, for a concert tour, of Liberace, with his mother and his brother.

This horrifying photograph was taken by John Sadovy as bullets from the rebels struck two Communist Secret Police during the Hungarian rising.

1957
Sputniks
Hula-hoops
and
Rock-'n'-roll

1957
Beauty of curves

Henry Moore, Britain's first sculptor to achieve an international reputation, working on a figure in wood.

Curves of a beauty

Jayne Mansfield (40–18–35) arriving at the Carlton Theatre, Haymarket, for the première of her film *Oh, for a Man!*

[41]

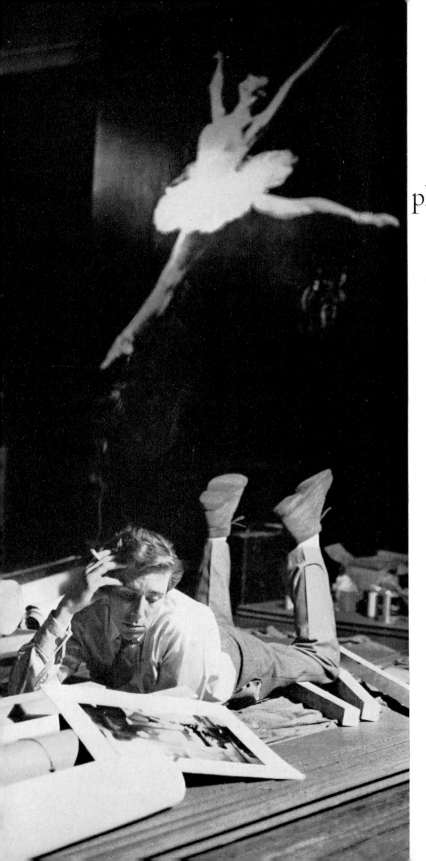

Rising
young
photographe[r]
plans an
exhibition
of his
work

1959

Bottle parties

The West Indian immigration into Britain is at its height. The gaiety of the immigrants is not always popular with their neighbours. Even less popular were the two hundred members of the 'Chelsea set' who barged on to the 8.3 p.m. Inner Circle Underground train at Sloane Square for a bottle party on wheels on 20 March.

1959 Bardolatry

1960 Youth, ah, youth!

Beatniks Jonathan and Sonia make a nice pictorial contrast to Miss Henrietta Tiarks and the Marquess of Tavistock. Below, two members of the

Ton Mob (a Ton = 100 m.p.h.) speed from Alexandra Palace to Ted's caf on the Southend road, where they will challenge each other to road-racing duels. Meanwhile, Dr Barbara Moore emulates Felix the Cat, and a 5-year-old Aldermaston Ban-the-Bomb marcher takes a nap.

PEACE NOT PIECES

1961 Space hero

Space chimpanzee 'Ham' grins as technicians remove electrical wiring and other scientific gear after his 420-mile ride through space on 31 January 1961. He went up 155 miles and travelled at 5,000 m.p.h. during the Project Mercury test flight, a preliminary to putting human aeronauts into space. Good for you, Ham! O Brave New World!

TWENTY-ONE YEARS OF
FASHION

by Ernestine Carter
with drawings by
Philippe Jullian

FASHION in Britain, like Sleeping Beauty, slept during the war and immediate post-war years, to wake at the Prince Charming kiss of Christian Dior.

Here is the look, which the war preserved, fly-in-amber-wise, long past its legitimate day. A legacy of Schiaparelli, its appropriately military air was perhaps not entirely accidental, for Schiaparelli took many of her inspirations from uniforms. The shoulder-bag, which was to become a part of the equipment of the American Women's Services, was presaged in Britain by our gas-masks, sometimes encased in suède (or, for evening, velvet) before they were happily discarded. Shoes and hair alike were practical, the first thick-soled, the latter slick-rolled—up, *à l'ange*, or under, 'pageboy' smooth.

[49]

1940

AS IF it were a tocsin of female emancipation, the first air-raid warning put the women of Britain into trousers. Slacks, in bright colours and patterns, had been accepted for holidays, and in velvet, *lamé*, or satin for evenings at home, but until the war Mesdames Garbo and Dietrich had had pretty exclusive rights to masculine trousers as everyday wear.

Trousers, both decent and warm, were of course entirely sensible and suitable for air-raid-shelter life, for A.R.P. posts. But, over-generous in the leg, too often over-stingy elsewhere, they suddenly invaded the streets as well. The All Clear has never sounded for them. Pipe-stem thin, topped with hip-length, baggy sweaters, they can be seen on any British street today.

Hair was a victim of the Blitz too. The dislocation of life and services transformed the crowning glory into a nuisance to be bundled away in bandage-like scarves or kerchiefs.

WITH the world in uniform, there were inevitable rebellions against discipline. The first sign of revolt was hair, which burst its bounds and rose to pompadour height in front, dropped to shoulder length at the back. In its most depressing form of uncombed frizzy 'perm', this hair-style became a headache to the Ministry of Labour, for the unrestrained fringes and the jauntily tossed curls were hazards in factory work. But, despite campaigns launched at official request by the women's Press and magazines, women once more proved their intransigence—and kept their curls. How many were actually scalped, history does not relate.

Perhaps as a reaction, other women, although keeping the pompadour, scraped their hair up on top of their heads, in a style dubbed 'Edwardian'.

Cold was an invisible enemy weapon. Blankets, or even evening coats, were commandeered to make house-coats or dressing-gowns. And boots were worn day and night, lined with wool or, for the lucky, fur.

1942/3

THE FRENCH COUTURE had been enabled to continue working in Paris during the Occupation through the efforts of Lucien Lelong, President of the Haute Couture, whose diplomatic handling of the Nazis dissuaded them from their plan to move the Couture to Berlin. But America, isolated by the war, had discovered and encouraged native talents. In Britain the members of the Incorporated Society of London Fashion Designers (founded in 1942) had reassembled from their various wartime services. The question was whether Paris could recapture her pre-war lead in the world of fashion (and, of course, her pre-war profits).

The answer lay in one word: DIOR.

FROM 1947 until his death in 1957 the magic name of Christian Dior dominated fashion. In his first collection his New Look, composed of heavily pleated skirts, dropped to below calf length, wasp-waists, accentuated bosoms (all achieved by elaborate inner construction), peplumed jackets, and soft, unpadded shoulders, changed in one fell swoop the face of fashion. And his dramatic method of presentation and astute sense of publicity changed the showing and the reporting of fashion as well. This modest Norman genius achieved what all makers and sellers of feminine clothing have always longed for: the complete overnight superannuation of women's wardrobes. Although he never again produced quite such a revolution, he reigned unchallenged for eleven years.

1948

IN FASHION as well as art Paris is a magnet for Spaniards. To Paris before the war there had come from a Spanish village on the Basque coast a designer who was to match Dior for leadership in fashion, and to out-live him. His name is Cristobal Balenciaga. Unlike Dior, he shunned and still shuns publicity. From his first collection in 1937 until today he has never appeared at any of his openings.

Remote, dedicated, and a skilled craftsman, he seems unaware of fashion trends, following only his own creative instinct.

But, although already 'discovered' by sharp journalistic eyes, he was not yet in 1948 the towering figure he has since become. Still, manufacturers also have sharp eyes and that year brought to England many copies of Balenciaga's long fitted torso and hip-accented riding-habit skirt.

COATS had become vast tents, un-belted, their flaring fullness swelling from narrowly sloping shoulders, but suits remained sharply fitted. Jackets shared the huge revers of coats, but snugly hugged the rib-cage and curved in stiffened basques over the hips. Buttons were many and bold.

Although skirts were still at mid-calf length, hair was being shortened, and a new cut invented by Antoine added to the hairdresser's vocabulary the word 'wind-blown'.

Balenciaga's pill-box began its perennial popular cycle, held on to the short-cut head by a veil.

While the smart world was muffled in yards of coating, Army surplus duffel-coats had become civilian uni-form for the young. With the duffel-coat came the habit of hatlessness, for ordinary hats looked odd (why, one wonders now, did no one take up the Tank Corps beret?). Another influence this coat was to have was farther in the future when top-coats began climbing above hem level. And the duffel-coat's kissing kin, the British Warm, was to have the same shrinking effect on men's overcoats.

1950

[55]

1952

'SEPARATES' had been the pre-war invention of Schiaparelli, who in quite another field shared in her hey-day something of the inventive genius of a more illustrious compatriot, da Vinci. Among her other innovations were the long dinner suit, padded shoulders, evening sweaters, eccentric buttons, and 'Shocking' pink.

Working in her imaginative Boutique was a talented young French-man, Hubert de Givenchy, who in 1952 launched his first collection on his own—a collection of separates. The success of his puffy-sleeved cotton blouses coincided with the rage for square dancing, and, with wide skirts, full or flared, out-held by petticoats, waists trimly circled by narrow patent-leather belts, flat-heeled ballet slippers, they became as epidemic in offices, on the street, as on the dance floor.

FOR less quaint parties the evening silhouette was fairly stable: long evening dresses were the exception rather than the rule. On short evening dresses skirts were mid-calf, their fullness sustained by many petticoats. Called 'ballerina', these skirts were an unbecoming length, long since foreworn by the ballet. Although the waistline was, in general, normal, a longer, slimmer torso was also seen, for in Paris waistlines had been skidding about and 1955 was the year that Dior launched his 'A' line, a triangle, widening from narrow shoulders, past a low waist-line, to a wide hem.

The 'A' line did not become part of the fashion alphabet and reposed quietly among the Dior archives until in Yves Saint Laurent's first collection, after the death of Dior, it reappeared as the 'Trapeze'. But Dior had still other surprises in store. In 1956 he made his unsuccessful attempt to drop skirts to just above ankle length.

This *demi-longeur* made head-lines but did not change hem-lines. Nor were women any readier to hide their legs when Saint Laurent in his turn tried to resuscitate the Master's premature change of direction.

ANOTHER fashion landmark this year saw was the chemise dress. Pioneered by Balenciaga, even taken up by Dior in his last collection, brought to dramatic popularity by Givenchy as the 'Sack'.

These changes were evolutionary. What was revolutionary was basic: heels had narrowed to stiletto slimness, to the ruination of polished floors to this day.

We were told that we had never had it so good, and in fashion we had never had it so mad. Here 1959 Dior (Saint Laurent) holds hands with 1956 Givenchy. In one you cannot sit down, in the other you cannot walk. During these years France and Italy were neck and neck in a wild race towards ultimate absurdity. Along with skirts, hair had reached new heights in a primitive shape called the 'beehive'.

1956   1959

THE EBULLIENT Italians, whose Alta Moda had been growing in strength since 1944, promptly transformed the Sack into what was irreverently dubbed the 'laundry-bag', and this zany fashion went quickly to young heads already light with enormous bouffant hairdo's, also Italian inspired. The original Givenchy sack was a triumph of clever cut, tapering to a narrow hem from width at mid-upper arm level: rather like a kite, in fact.

The laundry-bag on the other hand could be run up at home by any do-it-herself young thing. Perilously held together on bare shoulders, tourniquet-tight just below the knees, the sack became the dirndl of its day.

Stores could not keep them on the racks; letters were written about them to *The Economist*. Questioned about the Sack's figure-hiding propensity, sophisticated Frenchmen were quoted as saying that a shaded light was preferable to a naked bulb. But it was left to the more direct American male to kill it. And kill it he did.

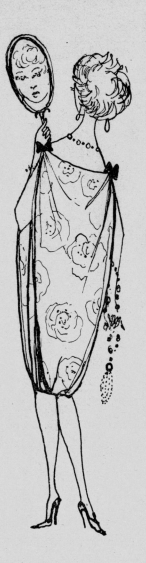

1958

1959

ANTI-FASHION can be fashion too. The Look, known as Beat, Beatnik, or Blouson d'Or, owes its origins to the Left Bank Existentialists and Brigitte Bardot. It was, in essence. an anti-Look: powder was white, lipstick so pale that it seemed non-existent; eyes were made-up to look hungover, hair was combed to look uncombed. Black stockings were essential and winkle-picker shoes, preferably in a pale glacé kid to dirty easily, with run-down spool heels.

Above the stockings there was a limited area of choice. Top favourite was an outgrown coat; next, a too tight, too short skirt. One accessory was vital: an unshaven, equally tousled beau in a mis-buttoned duffel-coat and shrunken jeans.

1959

CURIOUSLY enough, the anti-fashion of the Beats, instead of destroying fashion, produced a fashion of its own. In its most sinister phase it was dramatized and canonized expensively in Yves Saint Laurent's last collection for Dior. But long before this a young English couple had been designing clothes in the new tempo. Mary Quant and her husband, Alexander Plunket Greene, had opened a shop in Chelsea, the beat of the Beats. They sensed a new syncopation in clothes and have established a style, young, irresponsible, determinedly unserious, with its own language of accessories—patterned stockings, long-vamped shoes, dotty hats. Known in the United States as 'kooky', theirs is the first new British fashion to emerge since country tweeds and Ascot hats.

BY NOW Balenciaga and Givenchy had established a new proportion in suits: skirts were growing shorter to accommodate their shorter jackets. Sleeves were shorter, too, and revers fell casually away from loose, wide necklines. Jackets dropped straight at the back and were gently shaped in front. Buttons were big and braided.

But it is always necessary to remember that while the balloons and the hobbles make news, there are, in the collections of the great dressmakers, always wonderful wearable clothes. Our manufacturers buy both and adapt them to our needs, for these years have seen the rise of the British ready-to-wear trade to the point where, under the leadership of the London Fashion House Group, it is able to attract to this country buyers from all over the world. That is important from the Treasury point of view. From the point of view of our private treasuries it has meant that the British, as a nation, are better and less expensively dressed than ever before.

FASHION is contrary. No sooner did Balenciaga and Givenchy abolish sleeves than women rushed to bury their heads in the largest fur hats they could find or buy. Sable-topped or coney-crowned, a gathering of women resembled feeding-time at the Zoo.

Fur was the favoured trimming. Nina Ricci, whose new designer, Jules François Crahey, was giving new life to an old-established house, was collaring, lining, banding, and hemming dresses, coats, and jackets in rich furs. A clever American fur breeder managed to persuade each great Parisian House to use fox fur (bred by him) and the result was a succession of Nanook of the North hats, coats, and capes in lustrous black or snow-white fox. Mink and sable, for the first time in years, were worked with their strands running horizontally instead of up and down, a trick that uses more fur and gives appropriately a more opulent look. Only at Dior was fur treated with customary aristocratic negligence— there mink and leopard were given rib-knit collars and sleeves—*pour le sport.*

1961

THIS is where we came in. Here, after all the vagaries of twenty-one years of fashion, we find ourselves back to the military look of 1940. Here are the shaped jacket, the brisk shoulders, the inset sleeves, the jaunty pockets. This is Chanel's preview of the future.

In 1954 Chanel, whose name has the same legendary magic as Dior's, made her come-back after years of retirement. With a superb disregard for the direction fashion had since taken, she set about making the same sort of easy, light, simple clothes which had made her famous in the 'twenties.

Although one would have thought her tweeds exactly fitted English country life, we have taken a long time to realize their compatibility and are only just beginning to mass-produce the Chanel look.

TWENTY-ONE YEARS OF

Travel

ELIZABETH NICHOLAS

TWENTY-ONE years ago there was travel in plenty, of a sort, for those who were young. Rather peculiar travel, too; all expenses paid by His Majesty's Government, which undertook, what was more, to maintain the traveller once he had arrived at his destination. There was only one snag—the offer did not include guarantee of a return ticket.

But we travelled all right. Night after night Wellingtons and Hampdens waddled from dispersal bays on airfields scattered the length and breadth of England to claw their way into a painful night. One can see the airfields still, some of them, their concrete cracked and weed-encrusted, the broken doors of wooden huts flapping in the wind, mice nesting cosily in battered rooms where once young men sat listening to their briefing. These monuments to travellers of the early 'forties are with us still.

In those days great liners left Clyde and Mersey laden with brown-clad men, who might or might not return to Britain, the long day done. The liners lacked the amenities into which their owners had put such thought, such care, such prodigal sums of money; the interiors had been ruthlessly

E   [65]

gutted, and passengers swung on hammocks in vastly echoing dormitories. Still, it was a cheap way of 'doing' the Cape, the Indian Ocean, the mysteries of ancient Egypt. No one was paying a penny for the experience.

Across the seas moved the grey ships designed expressly to perform the functions that then absorbed them. Wardroom silver, accumulated through the centuries by other ships that had born the same proud names, was put ashore that it might find greater safety in a vault; paint, that might catch fire, was chipped from bulkheads; a few minor luxuries were cast aside. That was all; these ships needed no radical rebuilding that they might be suited to the type of travel we were embarked upon then.

A lovely sight they were too. I shall remember always a destroyer, long, lean, arrogant, as full of swagger as the proudest beauty, slashing her way across the South Atlantic. It was a day of brilliant sun, when sea merged splendidly with sky, and little waves were puffed with spume. I stood on the deck of an ancient Hollander and watched the destroyer cut, full speed ahead, between the lines of merchant ships that formed her convoy. All was grey and blue and white, save for the tiny splash of red that fluttered from her stern. The White Ensign, whipped straight by the wind, caught the throat as it passed.

Twenty-one years ago travel was full of moments such as this, when the destroyer that had, we were told, just sunk a U-boat, cut swiftly through the convoy, dipping as a ballerina acknowledging the cheers and adulation of a doting audience. It was a day to remember.

My first smell of Africa I remember too, the town of Takoradi, sweltering in heavy, humid heat. The smell of Africa—impossible to evoke in words, that musty, pungent, penetrating smell that has no counterpart. White people, I am told, emit a body odour that is disgusting to Chinese; we do not, of course, notice it ourselves, but we do notice the odour of other races. The African smell is strong, not disagreeable, but pervasive; I remember vividly the first occasion on which it penetrated my nostrils, eighteen years ago.

And Africa itself: the shanty town, the flaring lamps, the piles of oranges and grapefruit, then rare and half-forgotten luxuries, the men in ragged canvas slacks and homburg hats that had been sprayed with pink or blue or yellow paint; the flowers one could not name, the scents one could not identify, the sounds one could not explain—all living things that filled the evening air.

My first night in Africa was spent in Lagos, accommodated in an hotel

that could have learned a thing or two from Claridges. There I was witness to a scene that might have been lifted straight from Somerset Maugham; at any moment Sadie Thomson might have sidled down the stairs.

I do not know what lay behind it, what it was all about. I know only that I, and two other innocent English misses, sipping beer and harming no one, were suddenly hustled upstairs by the proprietor, bustled through bead curtains, and locked into an antimacassered sitting-room, whilst from below came sounds of crashing bottles, broken glass, scrunches, gurgles, and blows, suggesting that, somewhere, someone was indulging in a good free-for-all. What an introduction to Africa!

Across that Continent to Khartoum, to Cairo, and then across the desert to Lydda and the road that led in the end to Jerusalem. So I came upon that city for the first time, driving between olive trees and twisted vines, with men upon the road riding, very properly, their asses, whilst their heavily laden women walked behind. They were exactly like the illustrations in the Bible I had used at school; not a detail was changed.

Jerusalem, in the land then known as Palestine, I loved as much as any place that I have ever visited; as much as Paris, as much as Athens—I cannot say fairer than that. It was an enchanted world, warm, safe, secure from the storm that raged without. I try, now, to examine the texture of Jerusalem as I felt it, that winter long ago, but it escapes the questing fingers; I cannot pin it down. Those months were, for me, time out of war; I came with fifty months of conflict filling the immediate past, with Paris behind me and the flight through a country, beaten to its knees, that ended in Bordeaux; the blitz behind me, nights lived in the erotic stimulus of danger, war, and death, that caused the young to enjoy brief life lived fully amidst bombs and blast; the blackout behind me, the rationing, the tedium, the anguish, and the fear; and then Jerusalem the golden, lying still and cool and quiet beneath an immensity of stars. O Jerusalem! Shall I ever again experience such conscious joy?

In the spring, Beirut, Damascus, and a little inn, named with somewhat excessive splendour The Hotel of the World, that perched on the mountains above Chtaura. The fields were red with anemones, and we climbed up, up, beyond the snow-line, where little orchids pushed their heads into a chilly world. We buried cans of beer in the snow until they were iced, punched holes in the lids, and drank the contents lying in the sun amid the singing silence that is a part of all high places. At night there was a geyser to be fed with wooden chips from which, in the fulness of

time, belched steaming water grateful to the aching limbs. I remember it all, with love and longing.

The last year of the war I lived in Bari, and I wrote about Apulia for the *Saturday Book* of 1949. Apulia lay closer to me then in time, but not in my affection. That remains unchanged; the baroque and Byzantine south came as a blow to the face, so violent was its splendour. The vine, the olive, and the fig; carnations, lemon trees, and maize; the trulli houses where one golden day in February I picnicked on fennel, goats' cheese, and black bread, drinking a tawny wine; the fishing ports, the white-scoured rocks, the clams and squids, the luminous sea in which we bathed by moonlight, whilst, not so many miles away, the guns were thundering their joyless concert.

Time out of war: all lovely, soft, and glowing now, and dangerous. War will not be like that again, for anyone. One will not again swim in the afternoon with two young men and on the morrow learn that they have departed during the night watches on a journey from which they will not return. We shall, in the words of Rebecca West, all be despatched to heaven in the breachless unity of scrambled eggs. There will be no moments of piercing splendour to make one think, some twenty years on, that war was not without its consolations.

In a world once more pacific I sailed with my husband, whom I had wedded in the Cathedral Church of St George the Martyr in the See and Bishopric of Jerusalem, for Australasia. The P. & O. ship *Strathmore* still wore her war-time livery; as a colonel in His Britannic Majesty's Army, my husband was vouchsafed the luxury of a tiny single cabin, into which two bunks were wedged. Lying on the topmost of these I could watch in solitary silence dusk fall upon the Indian Ocean. Evening after evening I lay there, leaving the crowded decks to experience this miracle alone. Sometimes, because it was so exquisitely beautiful, I would find that tears were rolling down my cheeks.

We paused in Suez and in Aden, laying in stores of liquor, for the *Strathmore* was, officially, dry; after dinner we sat on cushions on the boat-deck, drinking gin from tooth-mugs. When that ran out one of our party succeeded in subverting members of the crew, purchasing for goodly sums their allocation of rum. I never taste rum now but what I think of the *Strathmore* and those nights on the Indian Ocean, when to sail openly, boldly, all lights unmasked and blazing arrogantly across the watery wastes, was a delightful novelty.

Australia—I have seen much of it now: Freemantle and Perth, and the rolling farmlands lying in the south; Adelaide and Alice Springs and Albert Namitjara; Melbourne, Sidney, Brisbane, and the coast of Queensland where rollers smash upon a sandy beach. The texture of Australia is, too, indefinable. It is a land moulded for idleness, where everything conspires towards a blissful nothingness. Who, in such a climate, with such seas, such beaches, could ever want to work?

Remembering Australia, it is the gum tree that stands foremost in the tablets of the mind. The brown-burnt country, heavy with heat, parched, imploring silently the benison of rain, is studded thick with gums that press majestically into the searing sky. I see them now, and the barbecue on Christmas night, when, on a portable radio, I heard the Festival of Nine Lessons and Carols recorded, half the world away, inside the grey cold walls of King's. 'In the beginning was the word. . . .' And it was the same word, for us and for our brethren whose lives were lived inside another hemisphere, twelve thousand miles from Cambridge.

What miracle of man's ingenuity enabled me to hear, lying in a garden beneath the Southern Cross, this festival of praise? The others were turning chops on the grill, opening bottles, splitting rolls; I was once more in Cambridge, shivering in a winter wind whilst the thermometer stood at 85 degrees and the tamarisk above me was still as death.

From Australia we sailed for San Francisco, and came upon the Golden Gates at midnight, eleven days out from Brisbane. The first glimpse of America—awe-inspiring moment—robbed of its magic by the U.S. Customs, who make no concessions to sentimentality.

We tarried in San Francisco, took train to Seattle, marvelling at the dark pine forests of the state of Oregon, fell in with a sea-captain in the Ben Franklin Hotel who warned us that Canadian trains were, like the *Strathmore*, dry, thus enabling us addicts to buy a quota of rye, and we sailed up Puget Sound to Victoria B.C. All, all was black and white and icy, for the month was January. My brother was born in Victoria B.C. but I had no time to trace his birthplace. We sailed again, for Vancouver, and found ourselves in a drawing-room on the C.P.R., pounding through the Rockies.

Then Niagara Falls, the spray frozen in the arctic air, and a train so hot that we had to sit in the guard's van to cool off; New York—Grand Central Station—driving down 5th Avenue. Oh wonder, oh splendour! What a moment of time! The skyline of lower Manhattan—*exactly* as one had imagined—how rare a travel experience is that—Greenwich Village, brownstone houses, shops with *food* in them. Shops with *nuts*; me, I am a fool for salted nuts and, because we were short of dollars, my husband would try to distract my attention whenever he saw that we were approaching yet another 'Tons of Nuts' establishment. Vain hope—I spotted it every time, and there was another dollar gone on roasted pecans, almonds, cashews.

Friends arrived on the *Queen Mary*; I remember a bar in perpetual darkness where we drank Old Fashioneds that we could not afford; 'making the economy'—buying delicious picnics from a delicatessen, smuggling them into our hotel bedroom; *Annie Get Your Gun* and Radio City; shops where one could buy clothing without coupons; the top of the Empire State. New York in the year of grace, Nineteen Hundred and Forty-Seven; the power there all right, but the glory dimmed. I did not find New York a pleasant place in which to live: exciting, stimulating, smashing, yes indeed, but pleasant, no. New York did not like me either. I did not envy New York its richness—well, not much; but I did resent talk about the frightful privations Americans had suffered that they might win the war for us. I had been in the docks during the Blitz and in the Apennines after the Germans had dynamited whole villages; and there were, I knew, worse things to war than being tightly rationed for gasoline.

My husband sailed in a blinding snowstorm for an England caught in the iron fist of a winter more intractable than any within living memory. In New York the snow was so heavy that he had to leave his taxi a couple of hundred yards from the Cunard pier, and, with the help of its driver, manhandle his trunk to the Customs shed. And I flew south to the sun. . . .

New Orleans, and a sudden shout of dazzling colour. My sister and I boarded a tram and noticed that there were seats to spare at the rear, whereas in the front people were standing. We went to the rear, and so came face to face with Jim Crowism. A coloured citizen, civilly enough, pointed out that, as whites, our proper place was standing in the front. . . .

Then the soft warm night of Merida, and Guatemala City as dawn spread its tentacles across the hills. Guatemala I remember as one of the loveliest of all earthly countries; the snow-capped volcanoes that slumbered fitfully beside the ice-blue lakes; the fruit and flowers, the oranges and lemons, tangerines and figs, the orchids, bougainvillaea, hibiscus, jacaranda, flame trees . . . all rioting together in careless grace, and the sun hot on the shoulders. The Indian markets, the pottery and bright-

striped blankets, water-melons, avocado, coffee. The smell of the coffee-sheds and the taste on the tongue of sun-warmed fruits, enclosed in a life of rich and sybaritic luxury. Oh yes, indeed, I remember Guatemala.

I remember also Belize; not, if I may say so, then one of the brightest diamonds in the Imperial diadem. My sister and I arrived virtually penni-less, all dollars spent; I arrived, also, suffering from a brief malaise. My sister rushed to a bank, there to draw on a sterling letter of credit; alas, it was a public holiday, in memory of one Sir William—Sir William—Bangs, was it? Anyway, he had, my sister was told, done much for Belize; what, she reflected, can Belize have been like before Sir William did his much for it?

Not to worry; the cook would lend us five (British Honduran) dollars. My sister emerged from the kitchen saying I could do as I thought fit but she was going to eat nothing but boiled eggs in that hotel. I saw her point, having just killed a cockroach six inches long with the back of a hairbrush; its remains lay squelched upon the floor.

Jamaica, the North Shore, then undeveloped, unexploited, no play-ground then for millionaires. An exquisite shore of silver sand and waving palms, of azure sea and darting fishes. James Bond still lay in the womb of history or, more precisely, in the fertile imagination of Mr Ian Fleming. Jamaica was, in 1947, heavenly.

The autumn of that year found me in St Germain en Laye, where I lived for several weeks with friends. Exactly twice as many years separate me now from that autumn in St Germain as separated me then from the Paris of 1940. Yet the seven years of exile from France had seemed an eternity and the fourteen years since 1947 have gone in a flash. I hold it still in memory, clearly detailed, that golden autumn when the war had ended barely a brace of years.

Food, of course, figured largely in the mind. The bliss of the thrice-weekly market: wandering round stalls of eggs and butter, cheese in rich variety, cream; the artichokes and small courgettes, the beans and aubergines, salads, endives; the peaches, melons, grapes, and figs; the butchers from whom one could buy *meat*, the steaks and fillets, chops, and escalopes, the kingly gigots. . . .

Oh yes, indeed, the food of France in 1947; and the Pernod drunk in the restaurant in the square, the moon falling on the shuttered houses, the Sunday mornings when we sunned ourselves and read the Paris scandal sheets. There was a texture to those weeks of mellow autumn that I shall

never know again; of being young and filled with conscious happiness, of knowing peace in a world grown sick of war.

In 1949 I became a professional traveller; and much wonder have I seen since then. New York again, and the Rockies in the month of May, cowboys and Indians in Calgary, snow by Lake Louise, steaks in Vancouver. Japan, and the curious excitement that was in it: a world that I could not enter and yet watched from the outside with awe.

I drove in pouring rain to the great temple at Nikko and saw a Japanese print alive in flesh and blood and clinging earth; the old men in the paddy-fields, with cartwheel hats and greying beards. Fuji, and my room in a Japanese (as opposed to a European-style) hotel by the shores of Lake Hakone, in which I fished for trout and bass. The room with fine-grained wooden walls, a lamp, a scroll, a single flower, at night a padded quilt upon the floor of rice-straw mats; a private garden filled with moss, azalias, a grey-stone lantern, conifers, and waterfall. My own private garden, giving out on to a secret world, and all the time the moonlight-flooded Fuji. Mysterious and untouchable, Japan entranced me.

I flew to Nairobi when Mau Mau was at its most atrocious worst: no fear I had experienced in war approached the agony of fear in Kenya when every shadow on the ground might herald death by panga. Never have I admired people more than I admired the settlers of Kenya then.

In Zanzibar the smell of cloves in the go-downs by the harbour to which the dhows had fled before the wild monsoon; the scimitar curve of white sand beaches, the fringe of palms, a singing silence; the Arab doors in the old city, the flame tree that shone in the garden of the Residency, the intoxicating sense that I was back once more in an Arab world, although the Arab world that I had known, ten years before in Palestine, had died and still awaited burial.

To Uganda and the Mountains of the Moon, the pigmies so educated in worldly ways they asked for cents and not for pennies. Elizabeth National Park, where, from the terrace of Safari Lodge, I watched, at dusk, three lions hunt a small gazelle, moving stealthily behind as it made its way to water. The journey from Butiaba up Albert Nyanza to the Victoria Nile; sleeping in the yacht and rising, at dawn, as it moved up the river to the Murchison Falls, with game coming down to the banks to water, elephants in scores, crocodiles, and hippos. The Falls where, a day or two before, Ernest Hemingway had crashed, his aircraft still sticking up in the bush a hundred yards away, abandoned, desolate.

I fished for Nile perch in Albert Nyanza. 'A pity you only got tiddlers,' said the captain of a paddle-steamer, as he gave my largest fish a contemptuous kick. It weighed but 57 lb.; a good Nile perch weighs around 250 lb. Ruanda Irundi, Albert National Park; sleeping in a round mud hut and shivering as the night was torn by terrible and unidentifiable animal noises; a rainstorm in the Ruwenzori, and right across Uganda again to the new Owen Falls power station, the mighty barrage, with memories of Speke and Burton.

Every country of Europe I have seen in this past decade. From Norway, beyond the Arctic Circle, to Istanbul that stands astride two Continents, the Sentinel of Asia. Cyprus, before her troubles were upon her—and us—and Greece during those troubles when the English visitor was treated still with exquisite courtesy; Madeira and the Canaries, the Black Sea, the Russian ports of Odessa, Yalta, Sochi, and Sukhumi that breathed a monumental tedium; Sintra in spring, Salzburg in summer, and Macedonia in the gusts of autumn. Paris at all seasons. Copenhagen when its copper spires were thrusting golden into a gentle sky; across the Mediterranean, Leptis Magna, more wonderful than words can tell. . . .

It has been a lovely life, and how well I understand my envious friends who cry in fury: 'Fancy being *paid* to live like that!' This brings me to my peroration: What does travel mean to one who is paid to undertake it? Is it still a wonder and a joy, a beckoning splendour?

Yes, a thousand times yes. I cannot say that the suitcase and the packing of it, the passport and the traveller's cheques, are still possessed of the delicious, tremulous anticipation that once they held. No longer does the coach from Cromwell Road or the boat train make my heart beat faster. But there is still emotion in a great express lying quiet beside a Parisian platform, in a silvery bird at rest in a pool of light on some far distant airfield, in a ship at anchor off a darkened shore. These things remain.

And, with them, a richness of experience, the joys of travel not diminished by familiarity but enhanced. The more one sees, the more one knows, the more can travel give. The new slips easily into focus; the old does not cease to play upon the vulnerable heart. Paris in the spring moves me now as it did those twenty-one years ago when, as a woman just crossed the threshold of maturity, I lived there through a winter of war. Venice still can sting the eyes to tears, and Athens fill the heart with wonder. Nothing can dull these polished shields, nor blunt these brightened arrows. Unchanged in a changing world, they still endure.

[73]

TWENTY-ONE YEARS OF

Films

DILYS POWELL

ALMOST the first letter I received on taking up the job of film critic was from an infuriated reader who, after reading my review of Alexander Korda's *The Four Feathers*, which I did not admire, as near as dammit accused me of sexual aberration. More than two decades have gone by since then, and for some years nobody has cast any aspersions on my hormones. I don't think I have changed, not, I mean, in that respect. But the public has changed. The climate in which films are seen has changed. The cinema itself has changed.

I don't want to bore myself to death with talk about trends, so let me begin with people: if you like, with faces. *The Face*: in his film Ingmar Bergman advanced the theory that the human countenance could be not only the greatest illusion but the greatest illusionist of all, and I am inclined to think he was right. The cinema is for faces: enormous, mesmerizing, bending on you their huge liquid eyes. The screen lives by them. At a first glance they may seem not to have conspicuously changed in twenty-one years. In 1940 you could have seen the young John Wayne

fighting off the Indians in *Stagecoach*. In 1961 in *The Alamo* he was still fighting off the attackers: Mexicans instead of Indians, and in colour instead of black-and-white, but it was the same face, a little heavier, a shade more lined about the eyes, but still John Wayne. In 1940 Spencer Tracy was already playing parts outside the range of the routine romantic hero. He is still playing them, and so is Frederic March. Two of the immortals, Garbo and Chaplin, are in retirement, and a few of the fabled figures have vanished. We shall not see Clark Gable in a new film again, nor Errol Flynn; Humphrey Bogart has gone, and Gary Cooper, and Tyrone Power. But James Stewart, Robert Taylor, Fred MacMurray, Cary Grant, Henry Fonda, James Cagney—their faces still turn to us from the screen, and to those who have watched while the pre-war generation has given way to the post-war they don't look as if they have altered much.

But in reality, of course, they have altered a great deal. Their shadows in the beam of the projector have lost their smoothness and grown older; and the flesh-and-blood audiences have grown younger. All cinema audiences are predominantly young, today more than ever; and the 1961 audiences want faces of their own generation. They are irritated by the persistence of stars from what seems to them another century. The older spectator himself can be faintly disapproving, especially if a celebrity from the 'thirties is romantically involved with an actress much younger. When Fred Astaire in *Funny Face*, when the late Gary Cooper in *Love in the Afternoon*, was paired off with Audrey Hepburn there was a growl of moral indignation. You might have thought the girl had been assaulted. And nobody, it seems, wants the character-hero any more—the scientist, the inventor, the family man who made the headlines in the 'thirties and the beginning of the 'forties. Before the war Paul Muni as Zola or Pasteur could draw crowds. In 1960 his appearance as the crotchety old doctor of *The Last Angry Man* was icily received, and I don't myself believe it was all the fault of the script, the direction, or the acting.

Looking back on the years of the war, one has to admit that the screen was full of stars then; one didn't at the time, perhaps, fully appreciate how brightly they shone. Especially that was a time for women stars, and especially American women stars. Claudette Colbert, Irene Dunne, Myrna Loy, and Jean Arthur were at the full flowering of their gifts; no national cinema has ever had such a band of comediennes to show. There was Barbara Stanwyck, a superbly confident player, though never given her due—others won awards, but not Barbara Stanwyck. There was

Ginger Rogers, her dancing partnership with Fred Astaire past its best, but her acting not yet formalized (I wonder how many remember her in *Primrose Path* and *Tom, Dick, and Harry*). Margaret Sullavan, Carole Lombard, Marlene Dietrich, Rosalind Russell, Mary Astor, Joan Crawford, Norma Shearer, Deanna Durbin, and the great bold-eyed queen of them all, Bette Davis: the charmers, the beauties, the topical sweeties, and the true actresses—some have died, some vanished, some have never withdrawn, a few have proved themselves durable. But twenty years ago they could be seen all in full blossom.

And there were the newly rising stars too, men and women; think of Orson Welles. *Citizen Kane*—written by Welles, directed by Welles, produced by Welles, with Welles as super-hero—arrived in London in 1941. Arrived? It exploded. Suddenly the cinema public was engaged in a private war. In the evening over the tables of the Café Royal friends wrangled over the style and content of Welles's film. Its camerawork, cried admirers, was completely original; old hat, done years before, said the denigrators. It was a profound examination of the mysterious human heart, insisted the enthusiasts; a pretentious bit of popular psychology, came the retort. And while the intellectual arguments raged, in the cinemas the audiences took violent sides, as they were to take sides two years later over *The Magnificent Ambersons*, whistling on the one hand and clapping on the other. At a time when, with entertainment restricted by war, almost anything on the screen would pass, the early Welles pieces excited such animosity that they sometimes had to be hastily withdrawn. Such battles over a film—and one which at the Brussels Exhibition of 1958 was to be included in a programme entitled The Best Films of All Time—may seem incredible to a younger generation. And there, I think, is one of the changes in the cinema. Films aren't for controversy any more. They may deal with controversial themes, but the public doesn't care, the public accepts. Love and rage and the true ferocity of argument have gone over to the theatre.

Not that many figures as controversial as Welles can be expected in any age, and I suppose one should count as more typical of the period such regular fellows as Alan Ladd and Gregory Peck, who in 1945 was showing his impeccable jaw in a film about a priest, *The Keys of the Kingdom*. (The priesthood has long been a vocation popular with the heroes of the screen, and Bing Crosby, Humphrey Bogart, Henry Fonda, John Mills, and Alec Guinness, to name a few, have been among the

eminent figures called; one is still waiting for Elvis Presley to join them.) About the same time there was a bit of a rush among the women stars to play nuns, and two interesting and comparatively new faces were seen becomingly veiled, Jennifer Jones in *The Song of Bernadette* and Ingrid Bergman in *The Bells of St Mary's*. But celibacy did not have things all its own way. Those were the days of the famous pairs: Greer Garson and Walter Pidgeon; Myrna Loy and William Powell; Jeanette MacDonald and Nelson Eddy; one might include also Judy Garland and Mickey Rooney, though she was to do her best work not as half a team but on her own (I am thinking, of course, of *Meet Me in St Louis*). And this is the moment to recall the most brilliant partners of all: Spencer Tracy and Katharine Hepburn, together in *Woman of the Year* and *No Love* and *Pat and Mike*.

But these are all stars of the American screen; in that first half of the 'forties the British recognized few others. Of Continental players they knew only the French, and of them only a handful: Gabin and Fernandel, Guitry who was to fall foul of the Resistance, melancholy-eyed Jouvet, Raimu with his solid, heavy-jowled Provençal look (though a few Londoners, a few film society members, might have warmed to the splendid gifts of the Russians, to Nikolai Cherkasov, perhaps, or to Massalitinova in *The Childhood of Maxim Gorki*). Yet new contenders were appearing, and from this country. There is a common belief that in the 'thirties the British produced nothing but documentaries about malnutrition and pest control. People forget the work of Hitchcock and Asquith and the beginnings of Carol Reed; and they forget Charles Laughton, Robert Donat, David Niven, Leslie Howard, Michael Redgrave, Ralph Richardson.

Some of the famous made their reputation in England: Laughton, for instance, in *The Private Life of Henry VIII*. It was in American films, however, that we were apt to know them best (worth noting that *Gone With the Wind*, one of the greatest box-office successes ever made in Hollywood, had Vivien Leigh and Leslie Howard among the names up in lights). Still, from time to time they all came back, and a good many of them stayed to become identified with the British screen. And new names appeared: Deborah Kerr; John Mills; Dirk Bogarde (a little later); and the quartet who for a short space were to stand for the novelette-cinema of *The Man in Grey* and *The Wicked Lady*, *Madonna of the Seven Moons* and *Caravan*: Margaret Lockwood, Phyllis Calvert, James Mason,

Stewart Granger. And then there was a major event. For years everybody had been saying that it was impossible to film Shakespeare. Suddenly, and I say suddenly because one had never really believed in it, there was *Henry V*, a blaze of poetry in action. It was Shakespeare, and it was cinema. And Laurence Olivier, who in America as well as in England, in *Wuthering Heights* and *Rebecca* as well as in *The Demi-Paradise*, had proved to be one of the international charmers, presently went on with *Hamlet* and *Richard III* to show that a man could be a great classical actor on the screen as well as on the stage.

One looks back on the years from the end of the war to the beginning of the 'fifties as the time when the Italians with the neo-realism of Rossellini and De Sica were coming back into the international field, when Anna Magnani was first admired (the famous Italian beauties, Gina Lollobrigida and Sophia Loren, came later). And that was the time when the English produced good cinema—and lost their shirts on it. The films were good all right. *A Matter of Life and Death*, *The Red Shoes*, *Odd Man Out*, *The Fallen Idol*, *The Third Man*; and the vernal, inventive period of Ealing Studios too, from *Dead of Night* and *Hue and Cry* to *Kind Hearts and Coronets*: we surprised ourselves as well as other people. Let's not go into the gloomy story of finance; anyhow I am trying, as I say, to consider the screen over twenty-one years not as a kind of rising and falling Bank Rate but as a portrait-gallery—and that lets out the documentary, which relies rather on poster-faces, on the proletarian-heroic and the picturesquely wrinkled, than on the mesmerizers, the mirrors of our dreams, which I am taking as the symbols of the cinema. By this time the additions to the gallery were growing scarcer. I am not speaking of the gifted, the notable player. Celia Johnson—whose delicate talents had been scarcely recognized at the time of *In Which We Serve* a few years earlier—gave in *Brief Encounter* a performance which was universally praised, and rightly so. But it didn't make her a mesmerizer. On the other hand her partner, Trevor Howard, with his intent, seamy look, joined the portraits in an audience's memory. And soon *Great Expectations* was to put on the screen a face which would be among the world-stars: the long, sad, mischievous, incalculable face of Alec Guinness.

There was another face to remember in *Great Expectations*—Jean Simmons: pert, big-eyed, foreshortened, very different from the darlings of the decade before. Perhaps one could say that the public taste was already showing a change. It is true that Betty Grable, still at the height

of popularity, had the beaming physical contours traditional in American sweethearts. But Danny Kaye now: exuberant talent, nothing particularly romantic about the looks, yet when he walked on to the Palladium stage the girls in the audience were contorted with delight. And Sinatra: who would have looked at that irregularity of high cheekbones and formidable eyes and called it a world-winner?

Perhaps in some of the new idols there was by now a reflection of the feeling for violence which rules the cinema today. Burt Lancaster, for instance, who first appeared in 1946 in *The Killers*: intelligent, an experimenter on the screen, handsome into the bargain, but the face is capable of understanding violence in quite a different way from the stars of the 'thirties. Or one thinks of Kirk Douglas, of Charlton Heston. And as the 'fifties began a startling new image printed itself on the public memory: a face at once defensive and touched with brutality. For ten years, watchful, its hostility towards the world only thinly veiled, it has held its spell: the face of Marlon Brando. And now I remember an autumn evening in 1956 on Sunset Boulevard, and the huge auditorium of Grauman's Chinese Theatre crammed with young people: jeans, pony-tails, check shirts. Silence as the film began: *Giant* and Rock Hudson and Elizabeth Taylor, the current romantic darlings, the bold and the beautiful. All at once everybody stirred. The face on the screen was half-hidden by a hat insolently perched on the bridge of the nose, but the audience recognized it; they knew its nervous, defiant look, the rueful smile of the eyes; it was their own kind of reckless look. James Dean spoke to the young generation, and for them.

Violence, recklessness, a defiance of the old rules of settled behaviour: that is the new mood of the cinema. It is a change, you might say, of temperature; it is there even in the musicals, in *Seven Brides for Seven Brothers* for example. It has been exaggerated by the cinema's need to compete with television, a need which in the 'fifties produced Cinema-Scope, Cinerama, Todd-AO, and the rest of the big-screen techniques, not to mention the short-lived 3-D. And certainly television is partly responsible for encouraging the big-screen subjects of the past decade: the Biblical extravagances, the trips into antiquity from *Quo Vadis* to *The Ten Commandments* and *Ben-Hur* and *Spartacus*. At any rate, say the film companies, you can't get all those extras, all those Israelites and Legionaries, on a screen seventeen inches wide. One mustn't, all the same, blame the domestic screen for everything. It may be argued that the

horror-films of the last few years were made to lure the teenagers away from the set on the hearth. But something more than television provoked the science-fiction series in the 'fifties: something in the air, something in the news, something in people themselves. And the changes which one sees today have been felt everywhere—except perhaps in the sphere of the Soviet Union, where although the grip of propaganda has relaxed, although the incidence of human frailty even in Russia has been accepted, criminal violence and juvenile delinquency are not yet favoured as themes for the screen.

The gentler aspect of the screen has not vanished. It is there in the humane comedies of Jacques Tati; in the serene faces of *Pather Panchali* and the rest of the Satyajit Ray trilogy; in the work of De Sica. But none of these truly reflect the nineteen-sixties. The films which speak for the times are the midnight works of Ingmar Bergman; one might add the magnificent but ferocious post-war Japanese cinema; and, of course, the young, rebellious products of the French New Wave. These may be for a minority taste, but they have the flavour of today. So have the recent cycle of Tennessee Williams films; and the oblique Polish school; and such British newcomers as *Room at the Top* and *Saturday Night and Sunday Morning* and *The Entertainer*. The change is all there: the social attack, the violence, the introspection, the questioning. And in today's faces on the screen one can see the same rejection of once-accepted canons. The new heroes of the English cinema are Peter O'Toole, Albert Finney, Peter Sellers, Peter Finch; the new international charmers are Leslie Caron, Melina Mercouri. The nervous and the intellectual, the kitten-faced and the student of the Method; Marilyn Monroe, Joanne Woodward, Shirley MacLaine, Giulietta Masina, Audrey Hepburn, Brigitte Bardot—we have come a long way since the smooth, glittering comediennes of twenty and twenty-five years ago.

Or perhaps I should say that the fashion now is not for stars but for rebels. One is glad to think that sometimes it is even for actors and actresses.

TWENTY-ONE YEARS OF

BUILDING

by Robert Harling

with drawings by

John Smith A.R.I.B.A.

HOW many decisive buildings are being designed at this present time? Anything as portentous as were Palladio's villas? Anything as revolutionary as Paxton's 1851 giant glasshouse?

Who can say? The trends and portents will be seen later. Certainly vast numbers of new buildings are ridding the world of many outworn and cumbersome old buildings, but most of the rebuilding on their sites is far removed from any architectural revolution.

Anyway, let us leave these questions to the *fin de siècle* pundits. Here, meantime, is a cross-section of buildings which have caused some modest architectural excitement and aesthetic commotion in our own time. In fact, all these designs were built during

the life of *The Saturday Book*, which, for architecture, really means the post-war years. Although architects (frequently disguised as sappers) learned a lot about stresses and strains during some of those years, they did very little designing—apart from bridges, hangars, and bomb shelters.

Whatever else we may say about these new designs—and many thunderous remarks are made—most observers would agree that many of the new silhouettes they give to our cities and suburbs are, at least, visually exciting. Could you, for example, say what kind of building heads this page? You would be wrong. It is a town hall for Aarhus in Denmark, which was designed by Professor Arne Jacobsen. This, at least, is a far cry from mock pilasters and keystones.

F

Philip Johnson House, New Canaan, 1949 (Architect: Philip Johnson)

Buildings for living

DURING the post-war years native American architects, aided by the theories and practice of a group of uprooted European architects, including Mies van der Rohe and Professor Walter Gropius, have designed many interesting domestic buildings, a good deal less individualistic than those of Frank Lloyd Wright, perhaps, but far more influential.

Small modern houses, from New Orleans to New England, have shown a lightness and authority of touch which seems to have eluded British architects, with a few notable exceptions.

This lightness and assurance is even to be found in recent skyscraper blocks, whether for domestic or

Edith Farnsworth House, 1950 (Architect: Mies van der Rohe)

commercial use. The apartment blocks on Lake Shore Drive in Chicago, designed by Mies van der Rohe, make most of the modern blocks of our time seem ponderously monolithic. Their influence will increasingly be seen in Europe in the 'sixties.

Lake Shore Drive Apartment Houses, Chicago, 1950 (Architect: Mies van der Rohe)

More buildings for living

AMONGST the few post-war houses in Britain which would hold their own in any international company is Farnley Hey in Yorkshire, designed by Peter Womersley, who, unlike most successful architects, continues to design houses. Farnley Hey is a small, sanely designed, two-storey, split-level house in a magnificent position, and is a complete refutation that modern houses are bleak and cold. Magnificent timbers and bright colours within make the house as cheerful as a spritsail barge.

Professor Arne Jacobsen, the Danish architect, who now has an international reputation and practice, also continues to design houses, several of

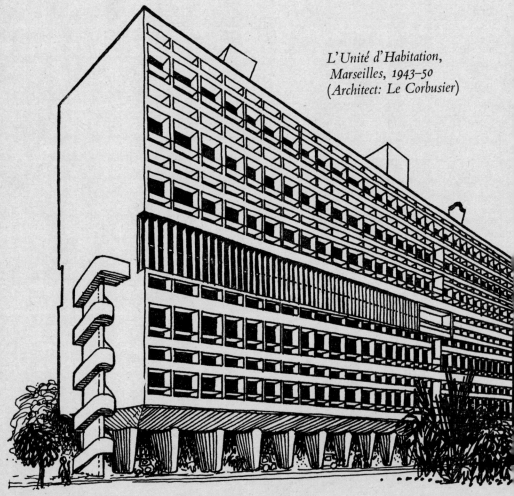

L'Unité d'Habitation,
Marseilles, 1943–50
(Architect: Le Corbusier)

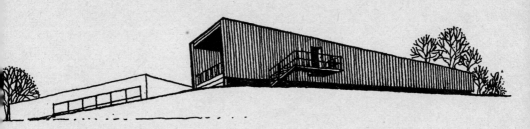

House at Vedback, Copenhagen, 1956 (Architect: Arne Jacobsen)

which have made a deep impression on British architects. The large house shown above overlooks the wide sweep of a Sound beyond Copenhagen, and its simple but dramatic brick-and-timbered walls around a triangular courtyard are a joy to behold. How fortunate, then, those future Oxford undergraduates for whom Professor Jacobsen is building the new St Catherine's College.

The Marseilles block shows what an eminent architectural theorist does when he gets his chance to build new flats on his own carefully worked-out modular principles based on that age-old rule—the physical span of man. Some critics contend that this block is little more than a concrete, dehumanized beehive, but the flat-dwellers seem to like their hive—which is something positive in favour of Corbusier's modular theories, at least. There must be other points in their favour, too, for other authorities —notably at Nantes—have similarly sponsored Corbusier blocks.

House at Farnley Hey, Yorkshire, 1955 (Architect: Peter Womersley)

Secondary Modern School, Waltham Cross, Herts., 1954
(Architects: Architects Co-Partnership, with C. H. Aslin)

Buildings for learning

BRITAIN'S post-war schools are equal to any in the world, a fact convincingly demonstrated by the Milan 1960 Triennale award to the designers of a prototype Nottingham primary

school which was built by British contractors in record time for the opening of the exhibition — after British officialdom had done its best to keep Britain out.

The late Sir Charles Aslin, the Hertfordshire County Architect (who died in 1959), did as much as any man to establish this leadership in school building, but several other British architects have notable school buildings to their credit. Unfortunately, the same clear thinking has not yet been noticeable in the admittedly more difficult architectural problems inseparable from building the new universities for future generations of British physicists and engineers. We shall see.

Architects in other nations have also produced many splendid new schools, although not on such a unified plan as those in Britain. This school in Rio de Janeiro (with new housing in the background) is typical of the spectacular designs of these new schools abroad. Let us hope their lessons of clarity and sound planning will not be lost on the fortunate scholars.

School and housing development, 1948–50, Rio de Janeiro (Architect: Affonso Reidy)

Buildings for worship

Coventry Cathedral, 1950–61 (Architect: Sir Basil Spence)

ALL ARCHITECTS, whether believers or agnostics, are highly susceptible and responsive to the subtle and complex challenges of building a new chapel or church, or, better still, a new cathedral. Ecclesiastical architecture has, throughout the ages, sponsored many architectural revolutionary theories. In no other division of architecture have so many conventions been thrown through the stained-glass windows, so to speak. And this tendency has been well in evidence in the church and cathedral buildings of the post-war years.

Throughout Europe new churches of unusual (and frequently astonishing) novelty in design have been built, often to replace structures damaged in the Second World War.

In our own country we have had Sir Basil Spence's highly controversial

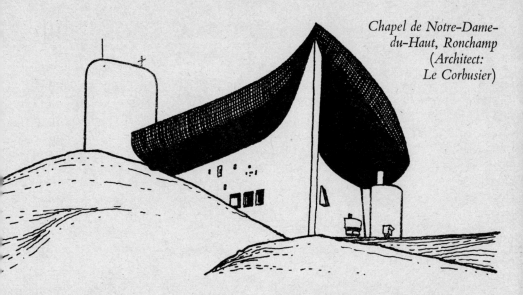

*Chapel de Notre-Dame-
du-Haut, Ronchamp
(Architect:
Le Corbusier)*

designs for Coventry Cathedral, consecrated this year, passionately defended by eminent critics and divines. We have Frederick Gibberd's recently published designs for Liverpool Cathedral. In Germany many new churches of revolutionary design have been built. But it is in France that the most spectacular new build-ing of all has been built. The Chapel of Notre-Dame-du-Haut at Ronchamp, designed by Le Corbusier, is a romantic, exotic, religious house, defiant of all known canons of ecclesiastical architecture, and, needless to say, multitudes of believers and mere sightseers crowd to see its novelties.

*Pirelli Building,
Milan, 1958–60
(Architect: Gio Ponti)*

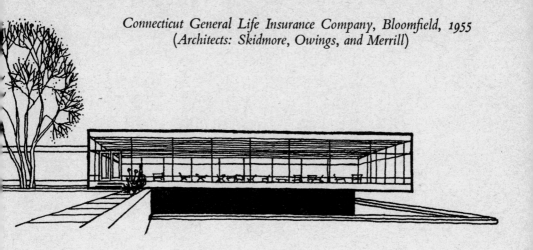

ıildings for working

COMMERCIAL prestige was (and still is, alas) too often reflected in overblown Corinthian pilasters, bogus keystones, and other useless architectural impedimenta. Dozens of recent office buildings in London show that this tradition is still alive and kicking hard. Will it ever die?

Yet a number of enlightened and internationally successful firms have shown that the buildings in which their executives and minions spend half their waking lives need not look like half-surfaced crypts or half-submerged mausoleums.

This trend is now well established in the U.S.A., and is to be seen at its sane and social best in the Lever and Seagram buildings in New York. Some American tycoons are also pioneering a new kind of office

architecture *away* from city centres, moving their headquarters out into smaller, less frenetic communities where lawns can be as much a part of the scene as cantilevered entrance canopies. The building shown above is an example.

Yet many organizations must remain in city centres, and Milan seems to be showing the world a new kind of commercial skyscraper architecture which is wondrously light and pleasant to work in, which skilfully avoids that canyon look of the skyscraper cities of America—and still provides enough prestige for any tycoon on earth. The Pirelli building, near the archaic Mussolini-inspired Central Station of Milan, is a most dramatic, pleasing, memorable, and efficient building. Similar buildings are arising elsewhere in the city, but they will never add up to another Wall Street. That is certain.

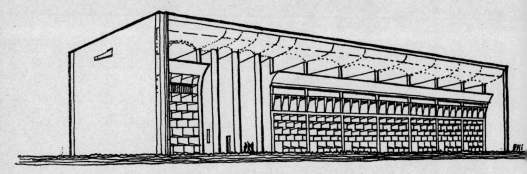

Law Courts, Chandigarh, India, 1958
(Architects: Le Corbusier, Jeanneret, Fry, and Drew)

Buildings for law and order

OFFICERS of the law seem to have an ingrained yearning to retain the sepulchral splendour of their nineteenth-century courts and corridors. Perhaps they feel more at home with these echoes of a less wilful, lethal, delinquent world. The Law Courts in the Strand, for instance, seem to reflect an awesome Victorian self-righteousness rather than universal, sempiternal truth and justice.

Yet a few forward-looking, optimistic planners believe that Law and Order in this splintering modern age can equally well be exercised and dispensed from buildings of our own time. Let us thank our lucky stars (and stripes?) that we have the U.N.O. building in New York looking as it does—a magnificent, glinting, slender, heroic, steel-glass wafer—and not like a colonnaded echo of the Parthenon or those strange relics still to be seen in Geneva. If there is any hope for international justice, then this kind of building attempts to house those hopes in a sane and courageous manner.

And in Chandigarh, that remarkable city which Le Corbusier is designing for the next two or three centuries of Indian self-awareness and advancement, a new kind of lakeside Law Courts has arisen which seems to reflect the authority and serenity which we all need to sense and *to see* in a Court of Law. John Smith's drawing shows the simplicity of the architect's elevation, but only glorious Technicolor could do justice to these great new halls reflected so tranquilly in the wide expanse of water.

Other nations, please copy.

United Nations Building,
New York, 1950
(Architect: Wallace Harrison)

The Sports Palace, Rome, 1957–60 (Architects: Nervi, Vitellozzi)

Buildings for beholding

THE ANCIENT GREEKS, to judge from visits to their ancient playgrounds, were fairly casual about their games: the spectators were part (or almost) of the general entertainment, as in a village cricket match. The more confining architecture of Sport (or rather spectating) as we know it today was definitively established in the Colosseum. Now sports palaces, stadia, domes, are here as part of each nation's urban scenery and international prestige, and the challenge to architects and engineers is irresistible.

What our forbears did so well we can do better! seemed to be the Roman war-cry before last year's Olympic Games, and certainly the stadia designed by that Italian genius, engineer-designer Pier Luigi Nervi, were both efficient and pleasing for looking from and at. They are portents. Already there is more than a whisper that the Chelsea Football Club will offer us a similar structure or series of structures within the next decade. And each nation vies with its neighbours for more splendid palaces of sport.

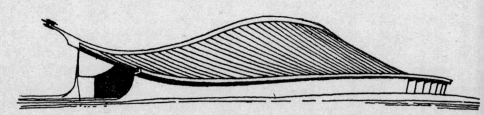

David S. Ingalls Hockey Rink, Yale University, 1959 (Architect: Eero Saarinen)

But not all onlooking is sportive in character. Aesthetic considerations will intrude. Coincident with the rise of Impressionist prices, for instance, has been a widespread interest in gallery-going. Nowadays tycoons seem to prefer to put their money in the paintings for their own private pleasure and for profit than into new art galleries. Fortunately, Victorian tycoons offered money for art galleries to be built. Fortunately, their old-fashioned legacies are still adequate for perambulating and beholding. For many years the clear-cut aseptic architecture of the Museum of Modern Art seemed all that an art gallery of our own time should be, and I always found it, paradoxically, a most exciting and restful place to visit, possessed, too, of that essential element in an art gallery—a decent restaurant. But now the Museum of Modern Art is old hat: the bespiralled walls of the Guggenheim Gallery of Modern Art in New York show what changes we are in for when our art galleries are redesigned by modern architects with ideas as exuberant as those of the late Frank Lloyd Wright.

Guggenheim Museum, New York, 1946–59
(Architect: Frank Lloyd Wright)

Naples Central Station, 1954 (Architects: Nervi, Vaccasso, and Campanella)

Buildings for travelling to and from

HOW can architectural technology hope to keep up with the inventiveness and dynamism of the aeronautical boffins? Nevertheless, a few notable attempts have been made to show that airports serve modern machines, even though modern travellers remain much the same kind of people that they were in the time of Herodotus. A number of splendidly imaginative airport structures have been built in the United States. So, too, in Copenhagen, Milan, and half a dozen other European cities.

Railway travel does not have anywhere near as many distinguished points of departure or arrival, romantic though they may occasionally seem. Most modern railway stations are woefully archaic, even in the U.S.A.

During the post-war years, however, Italy has built a number of remarkable railway stations which are magnificent and modern urban buildings as well as efficient administrative units. Rome and Venice have magnificent stations, but the most remarkable is undoubtedly that now nearing completion in Naples.

We are promised a number of new stations in Britain during the next decade, including redesigned Euston and Victoria stations, but we have all become disbelievers in the promises of the nationalizers, I suspect. We can but hope.

St Louis Municipal Airport, 1954 (Architect: Yamasaki)

TWENTY-ONE YEARS OF
Jazz
BY KENNETH ALLSOP

I N OCTOBER 1940 a retired saxophonist named Henry Minton, who was the first Negro delegate to Local 802, the New York branch of the American Musicians' Union, took a lease on a vacated and dilapidated room adjoining the Hotel Cecil on West 118th Street and reopened it as a musicians' club. He put in as manager Teddy Hill who, in disgust and in the red, had just dissolved his own band. Hill brought in as the Minton's Playhouse resident group three of his old sidesmen, including a brilliant young drummer named Kenneth Spearman Clarke, and also engaged a zany, wayward, bearded pianist named Thelonious Sphere Monk, who was twenty that month.

This inconspicuous enterprise, twenty-one years ago, on a drab Harlem side-turning between Fifth Avenue and Morningside Heights, had as dramatic a chemical effect upon jazz as had Lord Rutherford's 1919 atom-splitting experiments, and his realization of the dream of transmuting one nuclear element into another, upon science. Indeed, the fission and frag-mentation of jazz that has occurred since then looks in retrospect like the debris from the bomb that Rutherford's research inspired.

A jazz era closed when Minton's Playhouse opened. In that smoky and crowded laboratory a spontaneous crash-programme converted into practice theory that had been floating about unformulated in the New York night air. Modern jazz was born and baptized 'bop'. Not that the bop draughtsmen—mostly down-at-heel and down-and-out young musicians whose style was too eccentrically heterodox for general marketing—were

G   [97]

all premeditatedly setting out to build a new credo. Monk said later: 'Nobody was sitting there trying to make something new on purpose. It was a job, that's all.' Theodore Fats Navarro, the trumpeter, like many of those involved in the early work-outs, wrinkled his nose at the term 'bop' and the hullabaloo it later aroused. 'It's just modern music,' he said austerely.

Bop, as is all technical advance, was troublesome to established standards, irresistible and necessary. But, for all the astonishment one may feel at the career of jazz, at the growth in only fifty years of a racial group's regional dialect into a global Esperanto, it might as well be owned straight away that its aspirations both to self-improvement and to worldly success have landed it near to a sorry mess of disorientated collapse. At its coming of age this year jazz needs the combined therapy of psycho-analyst, surgeon and evangelist to make it whole in mind, body and purpose.

Jazz had sprouted around the turn of the century as a home-made entertainment, in vocal and instrumental form, among the black labour-ing population of America's Southern States. The pioneer instrumental form was later docketed 'New Orleans', the predominant town in which the blues, spirituals, work-hollers, and voodoo dances of earlier genera-tions of rural slaves were drawn upon by urban brass bands and bar pianists who imbued their own folksongs or current pops with jazz pig-mentation. By 1917, when jazz had become the indigenous Negro work-ing-class music throughout America, its more obvious 'novelty' twists, such as ragtime and syncopation, were already being lifted by Tin Pan Alley, and widely popularized among a titillated white audience. Yet, for all the energetic debasement, until 1930 the hard core of pedigree jazz remained lustily intact, and what had come to be defined as hot music flamed most brightly in the 'twenties, played with the ebullience and un-complicated dynamism of Louis Armstrong, King Oliver, Johnny Dodds, and their contemporaries. It had also been emulated by a nucleus of youthful white partisans, especially Chicagoans like Bix Beiderbecke, Mezz Mezzrow, Eddie Condon, and Muggsy Spanier, passionate disciples and dogged exponents of the authentic Negro jazz.

At the same time, jazz had been reformed, stuffed into a party frock, and dolled out with the frills and furbelows of such 'sweet' orchestras as Paul Whiteman's. It was in the 'thirties that the traditional small group playing free-wheeling, improvised jazz languished. The day arrived of

the big swing band going through a discipline of orchestrated riff numbers, with spots left blank here and there for the brief gymnastics of star soloists. This was by no means a totally sterile phase, for among the Negro bands then in action were those of Fletcher Henderson, Duke Ellington, Count Basie, Jimmie Lunceford, and Lionel Hampton, and, despite the slick, strident ostentation employed, such white bandleaders as Benny Goodman, Artie Shaw, and Tommy Dorsey produced some brawny, dazzling sounds.

Nevertheless, by 1940 the slickness and stridency were commercially in power—and also the dance-band, the crooner-vocalist, and the cute ballad. Bing Crosby and Perry Como were the mass-sale singers; Kay Kyser's and Harry James's were the mass-appeal bands; 'The Ferryboat Serenade' and 'When You Wish Upon a Star' were two hit songs of the year. It was against this rule of the wet and the winsome, from which the only refuge for the jazzman was the strait jacket of the swing band, that the conspiracy originated in that improbable revolutionary cell, Minton's Playhouse.

It could have occurred anywhere in New York about that time where there was a meeting-point and platform for the random young Negro musicians, drifting about Manhattan frustrated and restless. Jazz, it was bitterly felt, had been kidnapped and corrupted. It was static, either fossilized in the out-moded bouncy monotony of the ancient two-beat Dixieland, or denatured by the streamlined rigidity of swing. The impasse had to be shattered, and it was in Henry Minton's room that the barriers were sawn through at the legs.

Minton's was an open house for any musician with ideas to express. It was part debating society, part test-bench. Every night, after finishing at the more orthodox clubs and saloons where they circumspectly dished out the orthodox music required, those lucky enough to be working joined their jobless friends at Minton's for midnight-to-breakfast jam sessions. Often fifteen or twenty aspirants would be jockeying to take a solo on the stand. When Ellington's band was in town Jimmy Blanton dropped by with his bass. At the end of his session at Kelly's Stable Lester Young brought over his quintet. Other up-and-comers who were Minton's habitués were Charlie Parker, the saxophonist who wrenched from his horn unprecedented anguish and anger, Oscar Pettiford, the bassist who was said approvingly to make 'a big, fat, hairy sound', Bud Powell, who had the piano wires jangling like exposed nerves, and Dizzy Gillespie, whose radical use of the trumpet was apparent in the attack of the first explosive note. But the focal figure of these charged, rapt, all-night trials was Charles Christian, a twenty-one-year-old tubercular guitarist, who was then appearing with the Goodman orchestra at the Pennsylvania Hotel. Christian died eighteen months later, but it was the consistent presence of his ardour, his questing imagination, and the fluid blending of his electric guitar with horn improvisations that gave coherence and direction to the new thrust forward of jazz.

What was being developed at Minton's was first known onomatopoeically as 'rebop', from Christian's scat-singing of the phrases to the musicians he was instructing. Its shortening to 'bop' was defined ideologically as 'music of revolt, revolt against big bands, arrangers, vertical harmonies, soggy rhythms, non-playing orchestra leaders, and Tin Pan Alley; against commercialized music in general'. It was also put more flatly by Clarke, who gave as one reason why the obstacle course of complex chord changes was deliberately evolved: 'Just to keep the other guys off the stand because we knew they couldn't make those changes. That way we kept the riff-raff out.'

Bop was studiedly cultish, esoteric—and racial. It was at heart a retort to inferior white musicians who had parasitically exploited the Negro's music, and also a militant demonstration against 'Uncle Tomism'—a prideful rejection of New Orleans jazz which seemed to these young Negroes to be an inherent part of their history of enforced kowtowing. Technically, bop was a breakneck but logical reassembly of melody, harmony, and rhythm, and was characterized by the flatted fifth, the note which sounds clear and sour throughout and at the conclusion of a typical bop piece. This reconstructed framework was a liberation to the soloist imprisoned in the conventions of bands big and glib or small and clodhopping, if he was clever enough to master the new skills.

Almost immediately bop stimulated fierce antagonism. By the middle 'forties, when Parker, Monk, and Powell were growing fast in stature and influence, bop had boiled over the walls of Minton's and Monroe's Uptown House, another proving ground. It met its first resistance in the jazz world itself—the derision and outrage of the entrenched old guard. Even the painstakingly amiable Armstrong committed against bop one of his rare violences: 'All them weird chords don't mean nothing . . . modern malice,' he said indignantly. Condon snarled: 'We don't play our flatted fifths—we drink them.'

Still, bop was on its way, and the rippling staccato cascades were already becoming a familiar, though still foxing, sound to the lay clientele of the 'strip, clip, and gyp joints' which packed 52nd Street until they were razed in 1953 for skyscraper development, and in which some of the Minton study-group worked. It was also beginning to penetrate the consciousness of big-band arrangers and instrumentalists, and some of the less hair-raisingly startling phrases—or just those that could be grappled with—were sidling as gimmicks into orthodox performances.

Simultaneously, bop was becoming a public target for the sort of prim resentment that jazz had attracted in its early brothel-confined days. There was hostile reaction both to the bewildering 'out of tuneness' of the music and to the *outré* uniform of the bopper, the beret, sun-glasses, and goatee beard made modish by Gillespie. The word 'bop' became a handily snappy headline word, a portmanteau label for viciousness, neurosis, delinquency, dope, and hazily unspecified war-time treason. It was 'zombie music'; it was banned by a Los Angeles radio station; *Time* Magazine sternly denounced it as 'hot jazz overheated with overdone lyrics full of bawdiness, references to narcotics, and double-talk'. By the late 'forties bop had, as have other passing catch-phrases, such as 'Angry Young Men', 'beat', and 'rock-'n'-roll', become a generic term of abuse for all manifestations of youth and rebellion. Certainly, as customarily happens when any new bandwagon hoves into sight, a fair amount that was either feeble or spurious passed itself off as bop, and many records of that period were antic with the caterwauling of baffled but dauntless trumpeters panting after Gillespie's flashing runs. And, of course, in demolishing the old clichés bop furnished a replacement set.

Despite the noisy controversy that for a year or two made bop obtrusively blatant, it never caught on with the general jazz audience, except briefly in a smart way with those always tensely abreast. That is understandable, for jazz had until then been essentially danceable and whistleable, and now the method was—even when an evergreen like 'I've Got Rhythm' was taken as the basis of a flight of fancy—to play variations without ever touching upon the melody, the cats fastidiously pattering round and in between the broken bits. Nevertheless, although never fondly accepted at large, bop had a profound and transfiguring effect upon jazz. First, there was what Barry Ulanov, the American critic, called 'the really staggering fact that jazz did escape from two-bar statement and the swinging void'. Second, although by 1950 bop was dead as

a genre on its own—the line can probably be drawn at the break-up in that year of Gillespie's big band, when he said simply: 'There wasn't any work for us'—jazz was out in new country, with wide areas for exploration ahead, belligerently jaunty but secretly uncertain of itself. By 1955, although Christian, Parker, and Navarro were dead, many young jazzmen who had learned the music in the exacting Minton school or from its graduates had dispersed to lead their own groups and compose—men such as Monk, Pettiford, Powell, Miles Davis, Art Blakey, Percy Heath, Milt Jackson, and Max Roach, who were going to colour the next decade with the vivid, kaleidescopic glints of bop.

If the idea has so far been given that from 1940 to 1950 all the tributaries of jazz had been converging into this central stream of progress, that idea must now be roughly uprooted. Bop was the crucial event of these twenty-one years, for it began a new age of discovery in jazz. Those young outsiders in Minton's Playhouse in 1940 were metaphorically pushing off from the overtrodden shoreline of a musical Old World into an unknown Atlantic of atonality. Where their temerity led—and how the knowledge they gained was misused—we shall see later. Meanwhile, during the 'forties, a number of separate and old confusions had been aswirl on the jazz scene. The oddest of all was that while the Minton plotters had been working on the assumption that jazz must be plucked from the box-office and its swing-logged decline, and raised by intellectual effort to a higher plane, where it could again function freely but differently, another body of opinion had decided that salvation lay in the opposite direction—backward.

A sub-folkways movement had for some years been groping back through the mists into the primeval dawn of jazz, and these collectors of antiques with equal zeal sought the biography of, say, a long-dead stevedore who had played part-time trombone in a defunct Louisiana street-band, and scavenged junk-stalls for records like manhole lids made by obscure wandering Mississippi Delta blues-guitarists. The revivalists pushed their criteria of purity back beyond the Armstrong 'Hot Five' records of the mid 'twenties, beyond the preceding Oliver records, beyond the pre-First-War recordings of Bunk Johnson's Eagle Band, and thence to the legendary—but unwaxed—cornetting of Buddy Bolden, the New Orleans barber who died in a Louisiana insane asylum. The first serious attempt to re-create these lost pristine sounds was by a white Californian named Lu Watters, who in 1940 formed the Yerba Buena

Jazz Band, which, although it produced an arthritically stiff and stilted noise, did pursue an uncompromising fundamentalist policy, and attracted a large West Coast following from fans hearing this brand of music for the first time. In America the traditionalist imitators followed fast, including Turk Murphy and Bob Scobey—this at a time when Louis Armstrong was appearing with Hawaiian groups and Artie Shaw was adding a string section.

The ripples spread farther. In Britain, where jazz appreciation had been a serious student activity of small dedicated groups listening to cherished imported 78's in what were called rhythm clubs, participation began in 1943 with the formation by George Webb of a trad-group which played regularly at the Red Barn pub in Barnehurst, Kent. From this local labour of love proliferated the whole extraordinary spread of trad-jazz in Britain. The establishment of this foreign folk-art as the normal dance-music of today's teenagers has brought about the curious paradox of the commercial success of musicians like Humphrey Lyttelton, Wally Fawkes, Chris Barber, Ken Colyer, and Acker Bilk, who set out as cultural prophets and find themselves in the Hit Parade territory. It has also had the unlikely long-distance result of acceptance of jazz generally on both lowbrow and egghead levels (criticism in the serious Sundays and weeklies, and Third Programme treatises on Alabama chain-gang chants and obscure Edwardian honky-tonk pianists).

This ferment of a search for roots and refreshment at the original fount of knowledge included the foundation in 1943 of a Melbourne branch of the endeavour in Graeme Bell's Australian Jazz Band and such sad experiments as finding the veteran minstrel-show trumpeter Bunk Johnson, by 1942 toothless and long a rice-field labourer, and putting him on as a rediscovery, a kind of Stone Age survivor, for the delectation of sentimentalists.

While bop and trad were busy in their vastly separate fields, there was a third force making an even louder noise, the progressives. They were agin everyone. The trad or Dixieland bigots, said the progressives, were mouldy figs; the boppers were highbrow bores; the swing diehards had tin ears. The music that mattered was that being played by Woody Herman, Ralph Burns, and Stan Kenton. The orchestras were big and brassy, the arrangements florid but punchy, and a certain classiness was paraded by the introduction of French horns and harps. The numbers became suites, and had titles like 'City of Glass' and 'Artistry in Percussion'. Kenton was the particularly controversial figure, a man of both

absurd pretensions and crusading sincerity, who dexterously took bop harmonics, Afro-Cuban rhythms, Alban Berg and Schoenberg atonality, bongos and violins, and mixed them all into symphonic wedding-cakes.

Nowhere do reactions react so violently and to such extremes as in jazz. Almost as soon as the bop, trad, and progressive styles had superseded swing, the cool school were, with an understatement that amounted almost to loudness, setting about making their predecessors look dated and square. Togetherness, the quality of the bopsters, was out; icy individuality was in. Hotness was out; deadpan, subtle nuances were in. The big band was out; the chamber music ensemble was in. The followers were not rug-cutters or jivers; they were hipsters who carried undemonstrativeness to the point of stasis. The cool jazzmen abandoned the Left Bank bohemianism of dress of the bopsters, and wore clerical-grey high-buttoned suits and black silk ties. In their music the percussive beat was numbed, melody returned, and instruments were given the classical sound that jazz had hitherto scorned. Oboes, flugelhorns, and 'cellos contributed to the new, mild, mellifluous and often anaemic tinklings of the Modern Jazz Quartet or the murmurings of the Jimmy Giuffre group. It was in 1949 that the cool school may be said to have been founded, when Miles Davis gathered around him an eight-piece group that recorded some John Lewis compositions. The movement spread when Gerry Mulligan started his quartet in California in 1952, and the work of Stan Getz, Shorty Rogers, Chet Baker, Bob Brookmeyer, Tony Scott, and Dave Brubeck—almost all of them pupils of classical-music conservatories—began to reach the public.

But the cool practitioners and their Milhaud-tinted musings did not long have the public's ear. Again, doubts were seething, misgivings breaking out in a rash. Increasingly it was felt that the red blood of jazz had been thinned to skimmed milk, that the fundamental point and purpose of jazz—emotional expression—had been lost in the attempt to make jazz academically respectable by putting it into the recital room and the jazzman into a morning suit. The reaction this time emerged in the late 'fifties, when there became perceptible a reaching back to the blues, to the foundations. Nat Hentoff, the American critic, lamented that the average young jazzman of 1960 saw no farther back than Charlie Parker—he knew the repertoire of Parker and Davis as a student knows his textbooks, but he knew nothing of the origins of his craft, of Armstrong's Chicago years and the great Negro bands of the 'thirties, of the

blues singing of Bessie Smith and Billie Holiday, of the Kansas City era and the Goodman Trio.

In the intensely commercialized field of rock-'n'-roll Elvis Presley's amplified distortions of the blues drowned the wispy refinements of cool music. Pushed into self-examination, jazz has lately recovered some of its dissipated vitality. An obligatory quality now is 'soul', an earthiness and emotional fervour that has been resuscitated from the old gospel songs and the spirituals. It was noticeable last year how many albums issued by both established and rising musicians had the word *Blues* in the title—sometimes evident there but not in the content matter. After twenty years of being a dirty word—redolent with plantation overtones—the blues had been pardoned and admitted back into favour. It was partly because the reign of rock had put the blues, or rather a travesty of it, into general currency, but also because the Negro is becoming confident enough of his place in society to look back upon his history in America not with shame but with dignity. The odd thing is that, far from the Negroes as a whole being pro-jazz, they have been for the past twenty-five years prissily anti-jazz. When, between the two world wars, a Negro middle-class strove to establish themselves in the northern cities of America, part of their process of emancipation was to rid themselves of the music that they had engendered and which belonged with the slum vice districts where it had found its outlet. Now Negro youth is coming to jazz fresh and eager to fill in the cultural gaps in their knowledge of their race.

Unfortunately, while jazz has become socially okay, both commercially in various degrees of dilution and taken straight as a cultural piece of folkways heritage, conditions internally have reached an ironical crisis. There are about five thousand jazz musicians in New York, and in this shifting, spasmodic economic area nine-tenths are unemployed at any given time. Yet despite this huge pool of available men, there is a constant feverish beating of the bushes for new talent. The post-war advent of the long-play record is a factor here—the emphasis placed on a need for each glossy album to be the first exciting showcase of a new genius. The consumption of geniuses has become frighteningly high in the past ten years. Today jazz at almost every stage of its development (and regression) is represented by living musicians, which must be a unique condition for an art form in all history. From musicians of Armstrong's generation down, on one night or other in any week in some basement or opera house or bar, there can be heard the country blues or rent-party

boogie, Chicago style or funny-hat Dixieland, mainstream or power-house swing, West Coast cool or Oxford Street Storeyville, skiffle or hard bop, ragtime or miniature concertos, rock-'n'-roll or folksong. Yet within this profusion and richness there is endemic unemployment and instability. Men with unimpeachable reputations and the experience of years of hard playing scrape around for work. Musicians whose names are renowned the world over have to take casual gigs to pay the rent. Although such as Earl Hines and Coleman Hawkins and Jack Teagarden —all men in their late fifties—have managed to earn an uneven living all their lives at jazz, the experience of some of the younger musicians has been brutal.

As the artificiality of star-making intensified in the post-war period, so did the abruptness with which the stars were extinguished by the fickle switching of attention to new styles, new vogues, new geniuses. Stan Getz, acclaimed the top tenor saxophonist of the cool era, abandoned for good the cut-throat competitiveness of America for the calmer and more loyal atmosphere of Europe. Lee Konitz, an alto player of languid, thoughtful tone, and once highly esteemed, is never mentioned now in the jazz journals. Paul Desmond, for eight years the alto man with the Brubeck group, is today, although as accomplished as ever, considered *passé*. Gerry Mulligan, the baritone player who was one of the trail-blazers of the early 'fifties, recently told a TV interviewer: 'I'm already old hat. There's another generation coming along.'

This murderous discarding of considerable talents, to dash after the new fad, the fresh face, reached preposterous extremes as the 'fifties closed. Sonny Rollins, a tenor saxophonist who had battled doggedly to gain acceptance of his harsh, saw-edged tone and his perplexing thematic improvisations, had barely won recognition on the critics' polls (a high rating on which stimulates bookings in night-clubs and at festivals) when he was ousted by John Coltrane, another tenor man with an even wilder attack and more searing tone. Then arrived Ornette Coleman, who blew a white plastic alto sax like a tornado out of hell, and the adulation and the hosannahs swerved to him. In 1960, when Miles Davis had attained international respect for the elegiac lyricism of his trumpet-playing, a musician who talked to some Harlem teenagers found that they had long since written-off Davis as an old fogey; as for Gillespie, he was regarded as antediluvian. When Martin Williams, the American critic, in 1959 was auditioning for scholarships at the Lenox (Massachusetts) School of Jazz

he found that hardly any of the young candidates owned Parker records—
he was like a monument in a town square, formally honoured but largely
unnoticed.

Protests have been made against this neurotic grabbing at difference for
for difference's sake, at the organized industry of trend-setters and fashion-
fixers which seems to stretch from the record companies right through to
the *avant-garde* jazz-buffs. John Mehegan, the pianist, wrote a letter to
Down Beat condemning the Establishment of critics and publicists whom
he considered had ballyhooed Ornette Coleman on to the throne. He
condemned Coleman's 'artificial promotion by a small group of king-
makers', and cried: 'Musicians arise! Rescue jazz from the cabalists, the
metaphysicians, the hucksters, the ward-heelers.'

But the hucksters and ward-heelers have always had a half-Nelson on
jazz, for it has always had to submit to the grip of commercialized show-
business to earn its living. And it is important to bear in mind that jazz is
to the professional, no matter how much he feels a vocation for it, a
bread-and-butter matter—you will never hear a first-rate jazzman using
phrases like 'art-form' and 'preservation of integrity', no matter how
faithfully he may in fact have preserved his own integrity in contributing
to what does, after all, surprisingly remain an art-form, enmeshed though
it is by cut-throat business of a markedly shady character, a jungle of
agents, pluggers, night-spot owners, and Press agents. The amazing thing
is that, beset by these pressures and temptations, milked for its pop-music
potential, vilified and victimized, ignored and exploited, jazz has held so
long to its identity—a fact that reflects both the virility of the music itself
and the tough idealism of so many of its practitioners.

Yet now, twenty-one years after its first important transition, jazz is
ailing and floundering. Up to a point, the swiftness of its growth, its mer-
curial readiness to try anything once—and even, as with New Orleans
style, twice—has been implicit in its vigour and restless adventurousness.
Now, there are reasons bleakly to wonder if this restless vigour has not
skidded into a condition of manic neurosis. In this climate of hectic
anxiety to be new, different, arresting, a technique or a principle of com-
position has barely time to be put to the test before it is counted out as
stale; a young jazzman with genuine fresh ideas is either ignored or for
a while absurdly over-praised so that, unless he has exceptional strength
of character (and a private income), he has little chance of developing
those ideas to maturity and complete fruition. And jazz must face an

additional and perhaps graver danger now that it has educated itself to the point where it moves ever closer to contemporary classic music. Once already in those status-seeking cool days, like a scholarship boy ashamed of his working-class parents, it deliberately shut itself off from the nourishment of its sources and almost starved itself into extinction. The jazzman who taught himself on a second-hand trumpet by listening over and over again to an Armstrong solo on an old 78 disc has been replaced by the student who understands bitonality, clusters, and displaced scalic patterns, who digs the twelve-tone row technique evolved by Schoenberg and Riegger. But the question that arises is whether, having broken free of the constrictions of traditional harmony, he will still be playing jazz.

In 1926 Jelly-Roll Morton, the diamond-toothed Creole who claimed to have invented jazz down in New Orleans in 1902, used to sing:

> Hello, Central, give me Doctor Jazz.
> He's got what I need, I'll say he has.

Jazz may have had what Morton and his generation of sporting-house entertainers and their customers needed, but how could they have suspected just how much this honky-tonk hybrid really had—the seeds of a major industry, a minor art, a huge body of literature on its sociology, and a cultural language of unique universality? Would Morton have approved the elevation of jazz to highbrow exposition, the concert-room, and the college of music? Very likely, for, pimp and gambler though he was, Morton had the Creole's rather genteel snobbishness about all that Uptown black music ('a lot of blatant noises and discordant tones'). According to him, in his talks to Alan Lomax in 1938 before his death, he looted the operas put on at the New Orleans Opera House for his piano compositions. 'There is nothing finer than jazz music because it comes from everything of the finest class music,' he explained. Perhaps, oddly enough, he would now consider it is being returned to its rightful place.

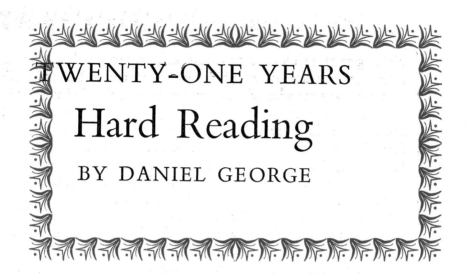

TWENTY-ONE YEARS

Hard Reading

BY DANIEL GEORGE

TO HAVE served, without remission for good conduct, a twenty-one years' stretch of novel-reviewing is nothing to be proud of. Having survived, I expect no congratulations. And I do not ask for sympathy. The experience has been, on the whole, enjoyable if not edifying or profitable. Bad novels mercifully soon fade from the memory. So, for that matter, do good ones, but not so completely. What's impossible to recapture, since I have kept no records, is my original impressions of such novels as I can now call to mind. Was I disrespectful towards specimens of fiction that other reviewers acclaimed as masterpieces? No doubt. It is equally probable that I overpraised the unpraiseworthy. Who now remembers or cares? An author here and there perhaps.

To believe that I have done more harm than good would unnerve me. (After all, my time isn't up yet.) I wish I could forget those lines by A. E. Housman:

> As I was walking backwards,
>   And never looked behind,
> I trod upon a lady
>   Who'd gone out of her mind.

But, of course, I am not proposing to walk backwards—only to go back and look forward. All the same, I must be careful.

A comprehensive survey of fiction published during the past twenty-one years would entail the re-reading of literally thousands of novels.

Nothing so thorough has been attempted here. I offer only a brief report based on recollection of some of my own private and professional reading.

In the war-time year of 1940 consumers of fiction had not yet been rationed. Novels written in the peace of 1939 (or earlier) were available, and minds could be taken off the immediate present by such recognized favourites as Hugh Walpole (*The Bright Pavilions*), Francis Brett Young (*The City of Gold*), and Compton Mackenzie (*The West Wind of Love*). This was the year, too, of Richard Llewellyn's *How Green Was My Valley*, and of the American John Steinbeck's *The Grapes of Wrath*.

By readers more discriminating, Rose Macaulay's *And No Man's Wit* could be enjoyed with Graham Greene's *The Power and the Glory* and Michael Sadleir's *Fanny by Gaslight*. Those public entertainers, P. G. Wodehouse and Angela Thirkell, had kept their customers supplied; and there was no shortage of whodunits.

In this period many people hitherto immune had contracted the reading habit, black-out restrictions and fire-watching duties having robbed them of their usual facilities for killing time. This sudden change in the intellectual life of the masses was viewed with apprehension in some quarters, and broadcasting wiseacres prescribed a corrective course of classics. Trollope and Tolstoy were exhumed. Such volumes of theirs as happened to be in print quickly went out of it, and the second-hand bookshops in Charing Cross Road were, it was said, exhibiting placards reading 'No Trollopes—No Wars & Peaces' to chime with the 'No Cigarettes—No Matches' notices elsewhere. According to unreliable authorities, the novel most appreciated by the troops was *No Orchids for Miss Blandish*.

In 1942 fiction could still have been labelled, in the fashionable term of reproach, 'escapist'. Lord Berners frankly appealed to 'escapers' with *Far From the Madding War*, and a refuge from reality was offered in novels by Elizabeth Bowen, I. Compton-Burnett, and Charles Morgan. Hemingway summoned us back to the spectacle of mortal combat with his story of the Spanish Civil War, *For Whom the Bell Tolls*, but of our own war the novelists had not yet begun to take cognizance. Crime stories were plentiful but concerned with civilians.

By 1942 a risk could be taken. J. B. Priestley's *Black-out in Gretley* dealt with some of the homelier English aspects of the world war. Hereabouts Paul Gallico's *The Snow Goose* took wing, and the first of the R.A.F. novels (later to be lumped together by the trade as 'wizard prangery') took off. Thrillers throve by occasionally admitting a spy to the story.

It is safe to say that before the end of 1943 fiction was *engagée*. Ehrenburg's *The Fall of Paris* was accompanied by C. S. Forester's *The Ship*, and Gerald Kersh's Brigade of Guards novels were in evidence. Most striking then, and best remembered now, Nigel Balchin's *The Small Back Room* (stylistically under American influence) set a new standard in laconic efficiency. A nice contrast to it was Rayner Heppenstall's disenchanted civilian-into-soldier novel, *Saturnine*.

Two novels of 1944 are not forgotten: Rosamond Lehmann's *The Ballad and the Source* (written as though in response to an anxious enquiry: What's happened to literature?) and Joyce Cary's *The Horse's Mouth*. Elizabeth Goudge with *Green Dolphin Country* and H. E. Bates with *Fair Stood the Wind for France* became best-sellers.

Of the 1945 output Evelyn Waugh's *Brideshead Revisited* and Aldous Huxley's *Time Must Have a Stop* were found the most praiseworthy. But the 'runaway' was the American Katherine Winsor's *Forever Amber*. Late in this year one of the first and most warmly welcomed of the post-war novelists appeared—P. H. Newby with *A Journey to the Interior*. Other new voices were heard—Nancy Mitford's in *The Pursuit of Love* and Elizabeth Taylor's in *At Mrs Lippincote's*.

By literary historians who go in for words like 'seminal' 1946 may be regarded as the year of Elias Canetti's *Auto-da-Fé* (translated by C. V. Wedgwood). Its influence is admitted, for example, by Iris Murdoch, whose novel ten years later, *The Flight of the Enchanter*, is dedicated to Canetti. At this time, among novels that called for less effort on the part of the reader, Eric Linklater's *Private Angelo* was in high favour.

By now the post-war period had set in, and that mysterious entity 'the novel' was again being seriously discussed in the customary terms: the influence of one writer on another was industriously if not convincingly detected, the influence (if any) of writers on readers ignored. Also in accordance with precedent, the popular novelists were denied (as here) even their right to be used as background for vague generalizations and vaguer prophecies.

Existentialism was imported, having been publicized by the novels of Jean-Paul Sartre and Albert Camus, but reverberations from its impact were not heard during this year of 1947, in which the most memorable novel was Malcolm Lowry's *Under the Volcano*. Reviewers' critical faculties, now sharpened, were employed on demolition work. Displacements from both exclusive and common esteem were effected. Charles

[111]

Morgan's *The Judge's Story* was not regarded as a masterpiece. Cyril Connolly's *The Rock Pool*, first published in France and now issued over here, was cautiously acclaimed.

War novels were beginning to pullulate. A surprise was the enthusiastic reception of *The Golden Warrior*, by Hope Muntz, which took no account of recent untoward events. Alan Paton's *Cry, the Beloved Country* —the first of perhaps too many novels from South Africa—made a deep impression on both reviewers and readers. John Mortimer, since famous as a playwright, introduced himself now (1948) with *Charade*, which made headway against the competition of Evelyn Waugh's *The Loved One* and Graham Greene's *The Heart of the Matter*.

Instantaneous recognition of his peculiar talents greeted Angus Wilson when his collection of short stories, *The Wrong Set*, came out in 1949. This was the year of Elizabeth Bowen's *The Heat of the Day*, Pamela Frankau's *The Willow Cabin*, and Nancy Mitford's *Love in a Cold Climate*. Italians gained a foothold here: Albert Moravia with *The Woman of Rome* and Elio Vittorini with *Conversations in Sicily*. But by far the most important novel of the year was George Orwell's *1984*.

Approaching the 'fifties, the reflective reader should have no difficulty in recalling the grave charges brought against the novelists of this decade or against the sum of their products. The indictment was founded on the allegation that in contemporary fiction the idea of romantic love had been superseded by the assumption that infidelity in courtship or marriage is reprehensible only in the eyes of puritans with nasty Freudian complexes. Further, it was suggested that good exemplars had given place to antiheroes, resulting in the apotheosis of the cad and the wanton—undesirables whom the post-war young would find it all too easy to emulate. By rejecting the traditional virtues, and regarding a sense of honour, or even of common honesty or simple gratitude, as an inhibiting, old-fashioned notion, the novelist—so it was said—enabled himself to dispense with decent restraint and achieve audacities that were, in the phrase of the day, great fun. But no Jeremy Collier who arose to denounce these modern Congreves could make his protest heard above the chorus of praise for sprightly exponents, on paper, of the 'new morality'.

As a non-literary judgment this manifestation of 'public opinion' was not without interest. The reading public was unaffected by it, and there was enough fiction about to which the stern moralist could take no exception. But the trend towards 'freedom' was noticeable and it is possible to feel

that now (1961) a destination has been reached. Meanwhile, the novel-reader of 1950 could find pleasure in Rose Macaulay's *The World My Wilderness*, Margaret Kennedy's *The Feast*, and Nevil Shute's *A Town Like Alice*. The new novelist of the day was Elizabeth Jane Howard with *The Beautiful Visit*.

The war at sea began to find its way into fiction. Nicholas Monsarrat's *The Cruel Sea* was rivalled by the American Herman Wouk's *The 'Caine' Mutiny*, the latter being remarkable for the fact that the author had sacrificed none of his 'realism' by omitting the profanity and impropriety of language by which a year earlier Norman Mailer in *The Naked and the Dead* had been instrumental in establishing a printers' precedent. Praise-worthy as Herman Wouk's achievement was, Norman Mailer's was the example sedulously followed in the American novels to come. Perhaps in England 1951 will be remembered by some as the year in which C. P. Snow, who had been plodding along since 1940 with what is called his 'Strangers and Brothers Sequence', got through to a larger public with *The Masters*. Among the English novelists who arrived was Gerald Hanley (*The Consul at Sunset*). Science fiction was given a lift by John Wyndham, whose *The Day of the Triffids* was thought to be sufficiently disconcerting.

American authors were prominent in the following year. *From Here to Eternity*, distended by Jack Jones far beyond the normal bulk of a novel, helped to make the strong-languaged G.I. a familiar figure in the fictional landscape. J. D. Salinger, Carson McCullers, and Truman Capote—Americans all—were appreciated by a small number of readers. A two-volumed historical novel by our own H. F. M. Prescott rather surprisingly appealed to many more. Angus Wilson's first novel, *Hemlock and After*, survived its initial reception. By connoisseurs of good writing and fine social observation William Plomer's *Museum Pieces* was suitably esteemed. The same could be said of V. S. Pritchett's *Mr Beluncle*. Anthony Powell's *A Buyer's Market* focused favourable attention on his continuous 'The Music of the Time' sequence. One of the earliest of the Jamaican novelists, Roger Mais, in *The Hills Were Joyful Together*, reached a level of literary ability and quality not yet touched by the other writers from the Caribbean.

The presence of American novels was again observable in 1953. William Faulkner (*Requiem for a Nun*) and Frances Parkinson Keyes (*Larry Vincent*) in their very different ways did not (except literally) carry as much weight as Mary McCarthy (*The Groves of Academe*). English authors who secured a well-attended hearing included Maurice Edelman (*Who Goes Home?*)

and L. P. Hartley (*The Go-between*). Philip Toynbee, continuing, with variations, the experiments begun in *Tea With Mrs Goodman*, salutarily puzzled us with *The Garden to the Sea*. A new type of thriller-writer broke through: Ian Fleming, in *Casino Royale*, producing his now notorious and apparently unkillable special agent James Bond. John Wain, with *Hurry On Down*, made good his claim to be noticed.

As though he had been waiting in the wings for a cue, Kingsley Amis with *Lucky Jim* stepped into the 1954 limelight. He has since been followed by a host of imitators who with less wit and humour seem determined to keep up the supply of novels about booze and bawdiness at redbrick universities. It can perhaps be regretted that the creator of Lucky Jim has not attempted to start a new vogue with a different kind of hero. A new kind of novel came from Iris Murdoch who in *Under the Net* demonstrated that fun and philosophy were not immiscible. On more conventional lines, *Bhowani Junction*, by John Masters, soon reached the best-seller list.

The new estimable novelist of 1955 was William Golding who, with a style to match his ideas, had written *Lord of the Flies*. From France came Françoise Sagan's *Bonjour Tristesse* (up to date) and Marguerite Youcenar's *Memoirs of Hadrian* (historical). The translation from the German of Robert Musil (already known for *The Man Without Qualities*) continued in *Young Torless*.

With *Anglo-Saxon Attitudes* in 1956 Angus Wilson could regard himself as firmly established. A similar sense of security might have been felt by Iris Murdoch (*The Flight from the Enchanter*) and Elizabeth Jane Howard (*The Long View*). Han Suyin, whose *Many-splendoured Thing* had been thought to contain a disproportionate blend of autobiography and fiction, reappeared with *And the Rain My Drink* and consolidated her position.

For novel-readers 1957 was made memorable by Rebecca West, whose *The Fountain Overflows* was published early in January. Laurence Durrell's *Justine* (the first of his Alexandrian quartet) lacked neither professional admirers nor private buyers. The big noise of the year was made by John Braine's *Room at the Top*.

During the succeeding twelve months the American invasion continued with such startling exhibitions of small-town *mores* as *Peyton Place*, by Grace Metalious, and *By Love Possessed*, by J. G. Cozzens, in which the *liseur comme voyeur* was lavishly catered for. But it was a Russian novel, Pasternak's *Dr Zhivago*, that 'everybody' was said to be reading. France sent us, notably, *The Law*, by Roger Vailland. Among an encouragingly

large group of new novelists were Elaine Dundy (*The Dud Avocado*), John Playfair (*Pursued by a Bear*), and D. A. Nicholas Jones (*Parade in Pairs*).

In 1959 the Book Society changed hands. The first novel 'chosen' by the new hands was Pamela Hansford Johnson's *The Humbler Creation*. Muriel Spark with *Memento Mori* gained the polite esteem and public favour that had long been her due. A further consignment of fresh talent was saluted in the persons of Robert Shaw (*The Hiding Place*), Alan Sillitoe (*The Loneliness of the Long Distance Runner* and other stories), and Simon Raven, thriller-writer for the unsqueamish (*Brother Cain*). The most talked-about novel was *Lolita*, by Vladimir Nabokov.

Presumably still being read are the 1960 'winners': *The Leopard*, translated from the Italian of Giuseppe Lampedusa, and *Lasso Round the Moon*, translated from the Norwegian of Agnar Mykle. But our native writers were not crowded out. C. P. Snow was at length awarded the distinction of a Book Society 'choice' for *The Affair*; Muriel Spark pleased 'everybody' with *The Ballad of Peckham Rye*; Eric Linklater's *The Merry Muse*, with many sly digs at contemporaries, left nothing to be desired. Colin Wilson tried his hand at a novel (*Ritual in the Dark*), so did the artist John Bratby (*Breakdown*). Other adventurers into fiction were Auberon Waugh (son of Evelyn) with *The Foxglove Saga*, James Barlow with *The Patriot*, and Lynne Reid Banks with *The L-shaped Room*.

Fiction of the present year, since the whole of it cannot be covered here, since also it must be within readers' memories, calls for nothing more than a reminder that in January the Book Society's 'choice' was William Cooper's *Scenes of Married Life*. A more serious and more widely read novel was Graham Greene's *A Burnt-out Case*. This contrast in matter, manner, and intention will serve to illustrate the extremes of traditional English fiction at the present time.

That in certain directions taste has changed—better perhaps say tolerance has increased—can hardly be denied. What, less than a half-century ago, would have been stigmatized as strong meat is now treated as though it were as wholesome as milk pudding. Sex, sadism, and crapulence are commonplace incidents. The credit (or blame) for the fact that large sections of the reading public (old and young) have been rendered shock-proof should probably be awarded to American novelists, on whom the prevailing influence seems to be Kinsey rather than the now out-moded Freud. Their excesses may in due time court a poetically just penalty, becoming as 'dated' and comic as the ecstasies of Elinor Glyn.

English novelists have hitherto had to be sparing in physiological detail and their upbringing has saved them from using blasphemy as a weapon of humour. The restraint, self-imposed or not, has been good for their art. They have acquired from their opposite numbers in America the technique for producing the illusions of 'pace' and 'shape', but the gain has been at the expense of what used to be known as good writing. A 'literary' style is now discouraged: analyses of emotions and displays of keen perception are deprecated. A Henry James *de nos jours* is unthinkable. Recently a slight recrudescence of proletarian fiction (fomented by writers who seemed, someone remarked, to be competing for a squalorship) was challenged by an outbreak of undergraduate impudence presenting, in 'pop' fiction too ephemeral to be deplored, the modern espresso café society.

At the moment among critics of the novel an epidemic of what Koestler once called French 'flu is getting out of control. From the other side of the Channel the *nouvelle vague* has washed up translations of the *anti-romanciers*. All technique and no tale makes Jean a dull boy, and it seems unlikely that English novelists will find they have much to learn from him in the process of creating reader-resistance.

Like Browning's Ogniben, 'I have seen three-and-twenty leaders of revolt—I have known *four*-and-twenty leaders of revolt.' It is not inconceivable, I contend, that the next leader may head a retreat into reticence. The wide diffusion of *Lady Chatterley's Lover* may result in the rediscovery that ridiculousness may be avoided by recourse to the powerful suggestiveness of three dots . . .

To leave the impression that English fiction is sex-ridden is far from my intention. 'The novel' is, as it has always been, healthily normal (light romance consorting easily with heavy allegory and stories of heroic action), but it is subject to occasional attacks of abnormality that may or may not be symptomatic of a renaissance of literary power. Comfort for guardians of the novel as a work of art may be found in the knowledge that there has been an enormous increase in the number of readers. Comfort, or cause for disquiet? Comfort, I conclude. Anyhow, the mercenary commencing novelist who aims low at the vast paperback public may find he has missed the target altogether. Standards are rising. Undisciplined energy abounds. The hungry sheep look up and are being fed. By whom? At the end of 1962 we may know.

Twenty-one Years of Wine

BY EDMUND PENNING-ROWSELL

'40 FOR MOST of us the wine years of the war are lost in the mists. Most of them were mediocre and small in quantity. The 1940 Bordeaux crop was poor and small, made under the eyes of the German troops, who were '*toujours correct*' in the châteaux they occupied, paid for what they drank, and despatched part of the population to work-camps or worse in Germany. The harvest was rather better in Burgundy, and some fair light wines were made, but few ever crossed the Channel, for by the Liberation they were mostly consumed or used for blending. 1940 was no victory year for German wines.

'41 A VINTAGE without a history, and fortunately, as a Bordeaux merchant remarked, mostly drunk by the Germans. The French hid or themselves consumed the better vintages. The Claret crop was even smaller than the previous year, and about as bad as the notorious '31. The Burgundies lacked fruit. For Hocks and Moselles it was a year to forget. In all the warring countries labour was short, and fertilizers and anti-parasite chemicals too. Only in neutral Portugal was some fair Port made, and of course bottled in Oporto, an operation which true-blue British vintage-Port drinkers view with disdain.

'42 A YEAR that had a certain amount of post-Liberation *réclame*, for it was being bottled just as the last Germans were expelled from France. Bordeaux made less wine than in any other war-time year, and some, especially the white wine, was good. Most of it went to slake the immediate post-war thirst for wine, but as late as 1960 I drank a surprisingly fine bottle of Ch. Latour 1942, probably the best Claret of the year; few others have stayed the course. The Burgundies were fair. Oddly enough, the very finest Romanée Conti that I have drunk was the 1942. Then about fifteen years old, it outdistanced, as it should not have done, the 1937. It was better, too, than the '43, which I have

also tasted. In fact, it was the last good year before this famous estate had to pull up its pre-phylloxera vines, which by the end of the war had almost ceased to yield. The German wines were better than for some years, but for obvious reasons were not exported. However, the Russians managed to make some very reasonable wine even in the year of Stalingrad, and I remember a 1942 Tsinandali, the dry Georgian white wine.

'43 HERE FOR the first time in the decade later to prove so fine we move into a vintage of some quality, over-estimated perhaps in the early post-war period, but a good year nevertheless. It was the best war-time vintage for Champagne, and for German wines too; some excellent but not very long-lasting white Burgundies were made. For red Burgundies it was the best year since '37; but the wines lacked staying-power. In fact, a tricky vintage to buy. Owing to labour shortages when due for bottling, as the war was ending, some of the wines were bottled very late. Some wine lay too long in cask, and lost its fruit and body. In Bordeaux it was the St Emilions and Pomerols, wines with an extra fruitiness and sugar compared with the more austere Médocs and Graves, that produced the best wines of the vintage. Ch. Cheval Blanc, the foremost St Emilion, made an excellent wine; so did its opposite number in Pomerol, Ch. Pétrus. Clos Fourtet was another St Emilion of distinction which kept well, as did some of the full-bodied Pomerols like Ch. Certan and Ch. La Croix de Gay. The Médocs were drinkable but often a little pinched. Ch. Pichon Longueville Baron was one of the best. '43 was the year we all enjoyed until the splendid post-war vintages started rolling in.

'44 A LIGHT YEAR, more notable in Bordeaux, where the largest war-time crop was made, than in Burgundy, where the vintage was rainy. So it was in Bordeaux, and quality depended upon the skill or luck of the proprietor in picking his grapes in a dry spell. Some of the *premiers crus* made unexpectedly drinkable wines. Ch. Haut Brion I remember almost as pale as a *rosé*. Latour was made of sterner stuff, and lasted well. No one in Germany or Champagne has cause to remember the '44s. A mouth-wash vintage to precede a great year.

'45 ANNÉE DE LA VICTOIRE, as the special neck-labels of the publicity-conscious Ch. Mouton Rothschild proclaimed. Even the cousins over the way, the less exuberant Lafite Rothschilds, had all their

bottles embossed with the year. *Le Bon Dieu* was on the side of the anti-Nazi powers, as the year of victory produced the finest vintage in France since the 1920s. Certainly a small vintage. Bordeaux, which usually makes about four million hectolitres of wine, and in the lowest war-time vintage had produced about two and a half million hectolitres, in this year harvested only 1,800,000 hectolitres—the smallest crop since 1915. Weather, manpower, shortages, and vineyard conditions all kept the *récolte* down. Ronald Barton, proprietor of part of the Léoville vineyard and of Langoa too, told me that weeds were rampant when he made his '45 wines; yet they turned out remarkably well. Both here and in Burgundy very fruity, firm wines were made. The Clarets still need keeping.

Not everyone in Bordeaux made great wine in '45; part of the Ch. Cheval Blanc was said to have gone wrong. The rival post-war vintage is '47, more forward, apparently more fruity, and sometimes surprisingly sweet. But not such a good keeper. The red Burgundies began to fail years ago, and the Clarets will not live as long as the '45s. These are softer now than a year or two ago, but those who have château-bottled '45s may be well advised to leave them until '65 at least. How much of their better-keeping qualities is owing to the fact that the post-war style of vinification, producing quick-maturing wines, did not come into fashion until after '45? The white Bordeaux was wonderful in this year, and in my view Ch. d'Yquem has not since matched its '45. The white Burgundies were excellent, and even the Germans made fine wine in diminished quantities. The French, it was alleged, removed a good deal to blend with their Alsace wines. Champagne had a successful year and so did Port. Owing to import restrictions this finest Port vintage since '35 was nearly all bottled in Oporto. Still, a wine to buy—and keep.

'46 ANOTHER SAD, wet year, which has left little of note behind it. There were in fact some reasonably good white wines, often less variable than the reds. A Schloss Reinhartshausen which I drank in 1960 was much better than anticipated. This was the last really poor wine year until '51—an unusual span.

'47 ONE OF the great post-war years, but uneven in maturing and longevity. The vintage came after the finest summer for years, not to be equalled until '59. In all areas the crop was large, in

Bordeaux particularly plentiful. But as in all hot summers great diffi-culties were experienced at the vintage; for excessive sugar in the grapes may easily cause the fermenting wine to turn to vinegar. A slightly acetic taste may be noticed when the wine has been in bottle for years. The successes of the vintage, and they were in the majority, were notable for their fruitiness and natural sugar. Although the red Burgundies have not stayed the course, some good bottles can still be found—and should be drunk up. The white Burgundies have not been surpassed since the war; perhaps the '59s will equal them. Without any false 'assistance' with sugar, they were—and when French-bottled may still be—wonderfully full of flavour and fruit. A domain-bottled Bâtard Montrachet '47 is the finest white Burgundy I know of today; fresh yet full, clean yet sweet.

The '47 Clarets, which were amazingly drinkable when I tasted them in cask in the summer of 1949, are still a subject of controversy. Perhaps the outstanding wine of the year is the Ch. Cheval Blanc: a huge, Port-like wine of extraordinary natural sweetness, still requiring time to soften its power. Alas, its sweetness has commended it to those with more cash than knowledge, and a great deal has been drunk already. The sur-vivors may well live to be the most celebrated Ch. Cheval Blanc since the '21. The Médocs, on the other hand, seem to me at their fine but not great best. However, the delicious '47 Pomerols provide for me the most agreeable of all bottles of post-war Claret, with great concentration of bouquet and flavour. I can recall a string of them from Ch. Pétrus, Vieux Ch. Certan, and La Pointe to lesser-known growths like La Croix de Gay. The white Bordeaux were good, and Ch. Climens headed the Barsacs. '47 Champagne was fine, and some very fair, quick-maturing German wines were made and drunk up. Portugal produced the most rapid-maturing of any post-war vintage Port, and with pre-war vintages now almost unobtainable, a good '47 like Taylor or Quinta do Noval is a fine after-dinner comfort. Southern vineyards, on the Rhône and in Italy, all made fine wine in '47, as they did not generally do in the similar '59.

'48 A YEAR unjustly dwarfed by its neighbours. After the fruity, bounteous '47s, the harder, less amiable tasting '48s were little bought for the English market either in Burgundy or Bordeaux. And soon the '49s arrived, widely hailed directly they were made. So the '48s were neglected. Certainly the Burgundies rather lacked distinction, although one of the finest of the post-war Domaine de la Romanée Conti

wines is the Richebourg. The Clarets, however, are on a different plane; for amateurs of true Claret, refined with still a shade of austerity in the Médocs, this is a year to treasure. Recently I have often preferred them to the '49s. Ch. Lafite made a very fine '48, and so did Ch. Léoville Barton. Ch. Cheval Blanc again had a success with a very big, fruity wine. Port scored too; for the first time since the mid-'thirties two adjacent years were 'proclaimed' as vintage years. A fine year also for Cognac, and in due course those few discriminating merchants who continue to sell vintage brandy will offer '48 Cognac.

'49 AS CONTROVERSIAL a year as the '47. But what would wine be like without controversy? Not the least depressing feature of wines from Australia, South Africa, and California is their usual steady 'success' year after year. At first '49 seemed to have everything: fruit, body, and depth. The white wines soon proved their merit in all the leading areas; the best German year since '45 and until '53; a fine full year for white Burgundies, while Ch. d'Yquem has not since surpassed its '49. The red wines, when first in bottle, drank well, but then they went into their shells, and were dumb and green. Some have stayed that way ever since. The Côte de Nuits wines are less soft than the Côte de Beaune, which now make delicious bottles. The development of the leading wines of the Côte de Nuits is certainly not complete.

The clarets are even more of a problem. Some experts say: 'Drink them up for they will never be better'; others, equally expert, say they show plenty of quality for improvement. The Médocs certainly are usually rather austere. The nub of the matter is whether the wine has enough fruit to outlive the hardness and, in wine jargon, 'ungratefulness'. My guess is that although the vintage has not quite lived up to early expectations, it will improve. Ch. Mouton Rothschild is generally acknowledged to be outstanding. On a lower level some of the minor commune wines, such as Moulis and Soussans, are more attractive to drink than the *grands crus*. '49 Champagnes were and are good, but they are now rare. In 1960 I partook of what must have been one of the finest and rarest Hocks of 1949: Deidesheimer Kieselberg Trockenbeerenauslese. It was said to have come from the finest cask of the German vintage. No doubt there are many claimants to such a title, but this wonderful wine—in the £10-plus-a-bottle class—had all the lusciousness of a great Hock, and had kept better than most German wines of the year.

'50 THE FIRST indifferent vintage since '46. Yet even in this rain-soaked year, in which the watery grapes produced vast crops, especially in Bordeaux, some excellent wines were made. Production was prodigious. At Ch. Pontet Canet, where about 250 tonneaux is an average *récolte*, something like 500 were made. The Médocs were inclined to lack fruit and be hard, but even here there were some surprisingly good wines. Ch. Lafite easily outdistanced its *premier cru* competitors, and is today a distinguished, elegant Claret. In Pomerol and St Emilion the quality was better, and they are good now. Were they a little assisted with sugar, illegally? Once again a medium-only year for red Burgundies, but some excellent white Burgundies were made. Few of the red Côte d'Or wines reached this country, and the Clarets owed part of their success to their low price. Oddly enough, it was a good year for both Port and Cognac.

'51 PROBABLY THE worst year since the Second World War. At last Bordeaux gave in over the matter of sugaring (*chaptalization*), and for the first time it was legally permissible to add sugar to the must; thus following Burgundian practice. Some said this was a dangerous precedent, but only an addition of sugar could raise the alcoholic strength sufficiently to produce a wine that would keep. Under such conditions some palatable wines were made, particularly in St Emilion.

'52 AFTER TWO indifferent years a loudly hailed vintage, for the wines had the body and guts which their predecessors lacked. Perhaps too much guts. At first, I remember, they seemed pleasantly drinkable for young wines. Then, rather like the '49s, they receded. Still today the Médocs are stubbornly hard and backward, and even the Pomerols and St Emilions, much easier to drink, have a certain firmness. Pairs of fine vintages are rare, 1899 and 1900 being the classic couple, and not to be followed until '28 and '29. The next couple are '52 and '53; and as on previous occasions each has its partisans. The Bordeaux view is that in '52 the Pomerols and St Emilions surpass the Médocs, whereas in '53 the reverse is true. Certainly '52s are *vins de garde*—keepers; and kept they should be. The same is true of the red Burgundies; they are firmer than the '53s, and, I would dare to say, better in the long run. This was the first year when the replanted vineyard of Romanée Conti produced a fine wine. The '52 white Burgundies were exceptional, with more quality than the '53s. On Champagne opinions differ, but '52 is possibly the better.

'53 THE SOFTEST, most agreeably forward red-wine year of the post-war period. The Clarets could be drunk with pleasure when four years old; supple, fragrant wines that have often been tossed off too soon. There are those who feel that a vintage drinkable so young must have a fault and will fade quickly. Bordeaux veterans will recall that this was a view widely held over the '75s—yet they were good after sixty years. It is a question of balance, and the '53 Clarets are beautifully balanced. Red wines often grow in bottle; they seem fruitier and fuller than they did a few years previously. Certainly the '53 Clarets are not fading—but they are being drunk up very rapidly. The most celebrated Claret of the year is undoubtedly the Lafite, a château which in many post-war vintages has often been *primus inter pares*, and has redeemed its indifferent reputation in many of the inter-war years. The '53 red Burgundies are less well balanced; the Côte de Beaune suffered from hail, but the Côte de Nuits escaped it. So the Pommards and Volnays are light and often less full of flavour than might be expected, while the Gevreys, Vosnes, and Chambolles are bigger and finer. Beaujolais had a notably successful year in '53.

'54 A YEAR without merit for table wines, with Bordeaux for the second time allowed to add sugar at the vintage. Some skilful blending with adjacent vintages and perhaps not so adjacent wine-growing areas produced palatable bottles. Ch. Cheval Blanc is unexpectedly good for the vintage. Some '54 white Burgundies were exported, perhaps 'assisted' by blending. Who cares? Only the purists. Some shippers made good Port; it all depended upon the lie of the vineyards.

'55 A FINE YEAR in all the French vineyards, in the Iberian peninsula, and in Italy; a fair one only in Germany, where poor weather at the vintage led to a lack of fruit in the wine. '55 is notable in a particular way for being the end of a line in St Emilion and Pomerol. For, a few months after the vintage, the most calamitous frosts in the history of Bordeaux almost wiped out part of the vineyards, particularly striking the old vines which give quality to a wine. So amateurs of Ch. Cheval Blanc, Ch. Pétrus, and other St Emilions and Pomerols have made sure that they have a stock of the '55 vintage; they are unlikely to regain their former quality until well on into the '60s. Excellent wine was also made in the Médoc and Graves, the last good year until '59.

It was a notable year for another reason in Bordeaux. It was the first

year when pre-vintage speculation began in earnest. From April onwards the unmade wine was bought and sold on the branch, *sur souche*. Even the *premiers crus* participated, but after '55 they agreed among themselves not to offer their wine before the vintage; advance speculation did not help their reputation if the wine was poor, and if it were a success they could obtain much higher prices after the vintage. To the regret of many the gamble came off in '55, and it has taken place in varying degree ever since. Burgundy, as growers say there disdainfully, has not succumbed to the practice—partly because vintage prospects are more uncertain in this northerly district; quantities are very small compared with Bordeaux. The '55 Burgundies are early-maturing wines and are surprisingly drinkable now. Some think they will be at their best before the '52s. It has been the most widely acclaimed Port year since the war. Champagne was fine too, but the quantity was small, as elsewhere in France.

'56 IN BORDEAUX the vintage was overshadowed by the February frosts. Ch. Cheval Blanc, which normally makes 400 hogsheads, made exactly two from its devastated vineyard. In June of that year I saw the dead vines in the Ch. Pétrus vineyard, looking like a landscape blasted by war. The Médoc suffered less, but the crop was small. The Sauternes area was badly hit. The Burgundy *récolte* was so poor that the Hospices de Beaune authorities took the unusual step of cancelling the famous annual sale, held on the third Sunday in November. This event provides the first opportunity of estimating the quality of the new wine. The prices, although not representative, for there is a charity as well as a publicity element about the auction conducted by candle-light, give an indication of the prospects. Some of the white Burgundies were better than expected, but, like the '54s, were probably 'assisted'. Altogether a year to be forgotten.

'57 AFTER the sad '56s, this year received rather more attention than it would have done otherwise. Burgundy was much more successful than Bordeaux, and the wines are firm yet fruity; experts suggest that they will be long-lived. The white Burgundies have a steely quality about them not to be found in the more supple '55s. The crop was again small, and at the Hospices de Beaune sale the prices reached an all-time record. The top *cuvées* fetched as much as £450 an hogshead, over 30s. a bottle while still in cask. The Clarets are hard, ungracious wines and so far lack charm. The German wines were dry and short in natural sugar.

[124]

'58 ONLY PORT established much of a reputation for this vintage, and it is certainly among the best since the war. In Germany the largest vintage of the century to date was made—of largely indifferent wine, whose best fate in many cases was, doubtless, to be blended in with the much fuller, but often rather acidity-short '59s. No doubt it was a useful wine for the 'manufacturers' of Liebfraumilch, that attractive, easily-remembered name of a generally over-sweetened blend that apparently accounts for 70 per cent of German wine drunk in Britain. In '58 Bordeaux produced some passable *vins de table*. Red Burgundies lacked distinction, but the white wines were rather better. Excellent wines were made in the Slovenian white-wine district of Yugoslavia; the '58 Sylvaners, Rieslings, and Traminers of the Maribor region can be delicious.

'59 THIS WAS talked into being a great vintage while the grapes were still on the vines. Partly owing to the exceptionally fine weather in the northern—but not the southern—part of Europe, partly on account of speculation in Bordeaux, and not least owing to the desire of the French growers and merchants, short of wine since '55, the '59s were talked home long before the grapes were brought home. The Press took up the vintage in a big way, and wine merchants were inundated with enquiries for wines long before they were bottled. A reaction set in; '59 was over-praised, it was asserted. What is the truth?

In Germany a remarkable vintage in the Rheingau and Moselle areas; the best since '34 or perhaps '21. Elsewhere in Germany a lack of acidity may result in rather flabby wines. Everywhere in Germany the quantity was large. Champagne had the first bumper crop for years, and in quality comparisons have been made with the '28s and the still more famous '93s. In France vineyard proprietors experienced the most difficult vintage since '47. In some cases, to stop the overheated must from turning to vinegar, ice-blocks were lowered into the fermenting vats. In Burgundy and Beaujolais some wine turned acetic, i.e. vinegary; and in Bordeaux time alone will show whether even in bottle some of the red wines will go 'over the top'. The quantity was small in Bordeaux, which helped to raise prices and assist the speculators, but large in Burgundy. At the Hospices sale very large quantities of wine from the vineyards owned by the hospital were offered for sale, and the total receipts were higher than ever before; but the price per cask was not so high as in '57. Undoubtedly a great year for Burgundy, that most difficult of wines to buy 'straight':

for 'sugaring', 'stretching', and 'assisting' with other wines is almost standard practice. Fine red wines were made in the Médoc and Graves, but some châteaux were luckier or more skilful than others. Ch. Léoville Barton and Léoville Lascases both made fine wine. Opening prices were astronomical, largely owing to the factors mentioned above.

'60 A YEAR that promised well up to July, and then was ruined by the persistent, ubiquitous rain. But the rain did mean an overwhelming quantity of wine in Germany, even exceeding the record '58, the first large crop in Bordeaux for seven years, and thin, light Burgundies and Beaujolais, appropriately described by one grower as *'vins de carafe'*. Yet such is the shortage of fine wines with a world demand that opening prices for these mediocre wines were startlingly high. Prices for the poor '60 Champagne opened higher than for the magnificent '59s. Indifferent Clarets were offered and sold *en primeur* for more than the '59s at the same period. The fate of every indifferent vintage depends to some extent upon its successor; if that is good, the earlier year is forgotten—or blended with it; if bad, the earlier year may be more in demand.

'61 LACKING THE crystal balls of Bordeaux speculators, I cannot confidently predict the quality and quantity of a vintage ungathered. After the poor '60, it will be approached with considerable optimism by a thirsty wine trade. Much ingenuity has been exercised from time to time in working out systems to show a pattern of vintages, but they have not been notably more successful than those for operating at Monte Carlo. In spite of expertise, science, and the Press, nature obstinately insists on having the last word. Therefore, to mention that the first years of decades have been particularly unpropitious for wine is probably to see the trend reversed in '61. Nevertheless, the 'ones' have produced some of the most lamentable vintages. '51 and '41 have already been discussed. '31 was perhaps the worst year of the century. '21 certainly was famous, but only for white wines and that red horse, Ch. Cheval Blanc. '11 was in fact a fine if little-known year. Ch. Margaux '11 is still a great wine. '01 was disastrous, and so were '91 and '81. Indeed, not until we go back to that mythical vintage 1811—the year of the comet—do we find an outstanding 'one'. Will '61 change the luck?

THE CABINET OF

Curiosities

ASSEMBLED BY

SEVERAL INGENIOUS HANDS

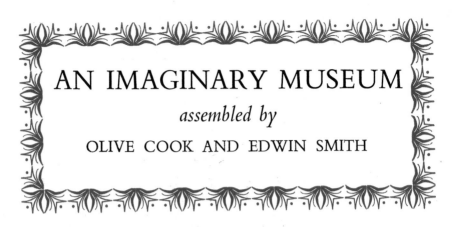

AN IMAGINARY MUSEUM

assembled by

OLIVE COOK AND EDWIN SMITH

THE MUSEUM from which these objects have been taken resembles the princely collections of the Renaissance rather than any modern institution. Nobody would think of it as a laboratory of research or a centre of public education; the contents are not disfigured by labels. Like the fabulous collections of the Emperor Rudolph or Cosimo de Medici it includes natural material as well as works of art, but, unlike them, the choice has been determined not by a predilection for the bizarre or the costly but by a passion for what is visually stimulating, whether it be found or formed, rare or common, worth a farthing or a fortune, a Titian or a Bamforth postcard, a fairground galloper or a horse from the palace of Ashur Banipal.

The Museum is not arranged according to period or category. Objects are grouped in ways which enhance their visual character and emphasize points of similarity and contrast in shape, texture, inspiration, and mood. Thus the visitor can marvel at the remarkably similar effects achieved by the application, for quite different reasons, of geometrical discipline to the female form as exemplified by a marble Cycladic goddess, wooden lay figures, and a stuffed fabric scarecrow. Or smile at a brass Britannia from a steam roller rudely aping the helmeted head and outstretched arm of an unexpectedly gentle Pompeian Mars. Or feel the excitement of fresh inventive ideas as he picks up a handful of beach pebbles, marbled, spotted, banded, like birds' eggs, like tabby cats, like watered silk.

The possibilities of the Museum can scarcely be conveyed in so brief a selection; its function is perhaps best summed up by the juxtaposition of the Victorian marble of a child and Paolozzi's head of bronze: it is designed to communicate a sense of the wonder of appearances and to celebrate the unique power of illusion not only to re-create the visible world but to illuminate the invisible world of the mind.

[128]

AN IMAGINARY
MUSEUM

'A Peep behind the Scenes':
Victorian lantern slide.

Below: Eighteenth-century
Russian sleigh (Victoria &
Albert Museum).

'Boadicea':
a child's shell
picture, 1957

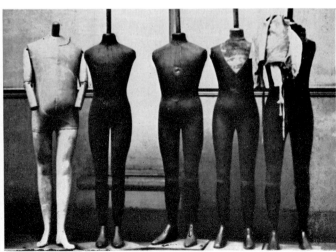

ove: Clay doll from Myrina, Asia
inor, first century A.D. (British
useum), and a modern Sicilian
ppet, Orlando Furioso.

1 the right: Wax dolls (Mrs Oliver
ll).

1 opposite page: Dress of the 'twenties
. & A.), a scarecrow, a nineteenth-
ntury tortoiseshell comb (V. & A.), a
cladic idol, 9 inches high, 3000 B.C.
ritish Museum), and lay figures
oulogne Museum).

ephord And The Philosopher
FABLE GAY

But he who studys natures laws And those, without our schools, From certain truth his maxims draw to make men moral, good and AP 17.

Above: Cut paper picture by Mary Parminter, 1742. *Below:* An embossed book-cover, *c.* 1840. *On the left:* Late nineteenth-century wallpaper (V. & A.).

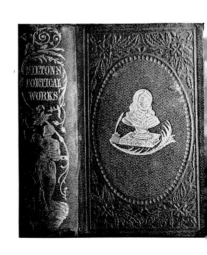

Above:
Victorian
still-life picture
in coloured felt.
Below: Porcelain
'Go-to-bed'
figure (K. Paul).

Overleaf:
Victorian marble
statue, *c.* 1870,
and 'Large
Head', bronze,
by Eduardo
Paolozzi.

Victorian earthenware jugs (Mr and Mrs Vincent Freedman).

Above: Detail of stained glass in St Aidan's Church
Bamburgh, *c.* 1880.

Opposite page: Japanese match-box labels.
Postcards by Bamforth, 1900–10 (Eric Barton).

THORA (4).

Speak! speak! speak to me, Thora,
Speak from your Heaven to me;
Child of my dream, love of my life,
Hope of my world to be!

WORDS BY KIND PERMISSION OF MESSRS. BOOSEY & CO.

She "Do you believe in signs"?
He "Yes certainly, whenever I meet
a pretty girl with money, its a
sign I'm going to fall in love."

Above: Modern bead funerary flowers, French.

On the left: Staffordshire earthenware figure, late eighteenth-century.

Below: Tombstone, 1792, at Wisbech, Cambridgeshire.

Above: Roundabout galloper, English, *c.* 1912.

Below: Assyrian bas-relief, ninth century B.C. (British Museum).

Pompeii: garden fresco in the house of Venus Marina, first century A.D.

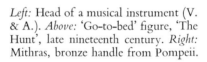

Left: Head of a musical instrument (V. & A.). *Above:* 'Go-to-bed' figure, 'The Hunt', late nineteenth century. *Right:* Mithras, bronze handle from Pompeii.

Below: Underworld demon from an Egyptian royal tomb (British Museum), and 'Britannia' brass steam-roller ornament.

Above: From an alphabet by Edward Lear.

Left: Stoneware mug with lid, mid-eighteenth century (Fitzwilliam Mus.), and a 'Poppy-head' in Acton Church, Suffolk, fifteenth century.

Opposite page: Water-colour by W. Hunt, nineteenth century (Victoria & Albert Museum), and Staffordshire bird-whistles, early nineteenth century.

Below: Construction of bird-bones and feathers.

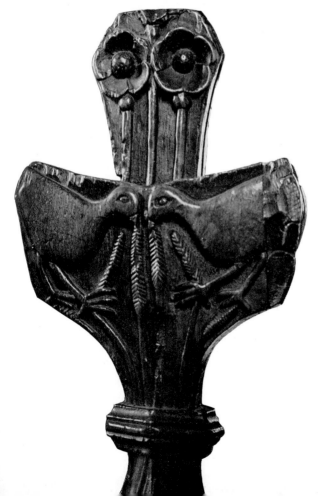

Fred Bason in Dawes Street Market, Walworth

LONDON STREET
Markets

BY FRED BASON

PHOTOGRAPHS BY
EDWIN SMITH

F OR more than thirty years I have been a dealer in the second-hand—second-hand anything, from books to cigarette cards. I have travelled to most street markets in and around London many hundreds of times, and I was myself for many years a seller of second-hand books from a barrow in a street market in Bermondsey. I have lived these past forty years in a colourful street market, Westmoreland Road, Walworth.

In the sixteen years I have been writing for *The Saturday Book* many hundreds of visitors to London have called on me and asked what they should see after they've seen the usual sights, from Big Ben to the Tower of London. To them I have always suggested that the street markets will provide all the colour and all the colourful characters they'd ever want to meet. So now it's occurred to me that a general guide to London street markets would prove helpful and amusing to *all* my *Saturday Book* readers.

The first thing I beg you to remember is that street traders are not fools; they are good business men and women. Don't expect to get a first folio signed by Shakespeare for 1*s*. 6*d*. Don't expect to get Ming for a dollar. The best bargain you will get in London street markets is genuine entertainment; and that 'for free'. In London street markets there is the best pantomime of life—and a pretty tough life it is. Pulling my

K

barrow-load of books from Walworth to Bermondsey, getting there at nine in the morning in a sweat, standing there in all weathers till half past two—well, it pretty nearly *killed* me. I know what a tough life it can be, and I also know that for the most part market traders are extremely hard-working folks and extremely *honest* folks. Of course, there are bargains to be had in some markets: no one knows everything, and even experts can make mistakes; but it don't often happen. Be prepared to pay a fair price for what you buy.

There are eighty or so street markets in and close to London. More than twenty-five thousand Londoners make their livings as street traders, and some of the most genuine of Cockneys can be found behind barrows. It's rather a curious thing, but over long years I've found that the most colourful of street traders are fishmongers . . . and next to them sellers of old clothes. The music of markets is irresistible, and the cries of the sellers as they call out their wonderful bargains always hold me spellbound.

I've put at the top of my list the Caledonian Market in Bermondsey, because for the visitor it's by far the most colourful, and everything is sold there. But hold tight to your purse strings; they have a wonderful way in Bermondsey of parting you from your money. Petticoat Lane is a more famous market, but it comes farther down my list because it's at its best on Sunday mornings, and not everyone is inclined to get up and make an hour's journey on a Sunday. But if you do I promise you a feast of odd characters, endless fun, and fascinating vocal music. There is no place quite like it; but be warned: you could lose your watch at one end of it and buy it back at the other end—if you've any money by the time you reach the other end. Many of the folks in this area of London are very rich folks, and the car they go out in on Mondays is much finer than your own.

I've walked along East Street Market, Walworth, at least three times a week for the past forty years. It's one of the markets that has never lacked colour. Its traders are particularly honest and the goods for sale are excellent value; this cannot be said for every street market in London.

I am greatly indebted to a book called *The Street Markets of London* by Mary Benedetta. It was published in 1936 and is now rare. It's the finest book ever on the markets of London, but, alas, it's now entirely out-of-date. Many of the markets no longer exist, and others have changed their names or their character.

The list that follows is probably the fullest and most up-to-date that

will be compiled for some time. If you visited all these markets in a couple of months you'd wear out at least two pairs of shoes. But you'd have seen London and its folk better than any guide or any travel agency could present them to you. The very few markets that are not listed here are really not worth your time or trouble since they would be a repetition of those in the list.

Bear in mind that it's a waste of time to go to many of these markets on a Monday. That's the day the sellers go out in their cars and smoke their excellent cigars. On the whole the best two days to visit markets are Fridays and Saturdays. But there are some exceptions. I've found over thirty years that East Street and Lower Marsh markets are brisk and lively on Thursday *mornings*, though quite dead by two on that day.

You don't have to be a visitor to London in order to get a great deal of pleasure in visiting these markets. Hundreds of thousands of Londoners don't know a third of them. As one market dies out in a small street—perhaps it's pulled down for rebuilding slums—then a fresh one opens nearby. And good luck to them all. The street-market traders are the salt of London.

I suggest that you make the point of starting every journey from opposite Big Ben on the corner of the Embankment, because there are many bus-stops, an Underground station, and (if you are rich) it's a very good place to obtain a taxi. By one of these methods you can reach all the markets listed. I have put them in order of interest, not in order of neighbourhood or nearness to the big clock. The best and the most colourful are the one's shown in Edwin Smith's pictures.

RUPERT STREET, off Shaftesbury Avenue, with the Globe Theatre on one corner. A tightly packed street market, busy and breezy, full of life. You go through it to get to Berwick Market, but it's worth a visit in its own right as a superb specimen of a London food and fruit market.

NORTH END ROAD, Walham Green. Go by Underground to Walham Green, and it's close by. A working-class market, mainly food, but very good value. Has many odd characters amongst its traders. Best day for a visit is Saturdays between one and four. No market on Sundays.

HAMMERSMITH MARKET, off King Street, Hammersmith. Can be reached by Underground. A neat and busy market, rather on the lines of Rupert

[147]

Street, but the street cries are at times most odd. It's rather a middle-class market, but it has much colour. At its best on Saturday afternoons.

LOWER MARSH, Lambeth. This market is just across Westminster Bridge and you can walk there in less than ten minutes. It has strangely assorted wares and a weird variety of stall-holders. It's very working-class, and at its best between twelve-thirty and two-thirty. Tightly packed every day. Go on Fridays and Saturdays.

THE NEW CUT, Lambeth. Starts beside the corner of the Old Vic. It is really a continuation of Lower Marsh. A sad market, with many gaps, for it's a dying market. However, many of the stall-holders are true Cockneys.

CHOUMERT ROAD, Peckham. This can be reached on a Number 12 bus from Big Ben, and is very lively on Saturdays. You go down Rye Lane and get off at the Railway Bridge. The market is but a few steps forward from the bridge. It's very much a working-class market, and sells pretty well everything. There is also close-by a strange covered-in market that's worth a visit. Extremely honest traders, and a very nice collection of Cockney stall-holders.

EXMOUTH MARKET, Finsbury. After visiting Farringdon Market continue up the road over Clerkenwell Road, and on the right you'll find Exmouth Street and a typical London street market, mainly food and household goods, but full of colour. It's in the borough of Finsbury, where you'll find other and smaller markets dotted around.

WESTMORELAND ROAD, Walworth. Four turnings past East Street Market, still along the Walworth Road, you'll find this market, with a pub on the corner. I've lived in this road for more than forty years. It sells everything, but these days it is mainly devoted to food and fruit. You will find the traders to be genuine Cockneys with a lingo all of their own. It's at its liveliest from noon till about two on Saturday. If you visit this market you are welcome to call on me at No. 152 and have a chat and a cup of tea on any Thursday. Thursday is my At-Home Day. Market open every day, but best day is undoubtedly Saturday. Dead on Mondays, as it opens Sundays as well.

EAST STREET, in Walworth. This is open every day except Mondays, but best days are Thursday mornings and Saturday afternoons. A genuine working-class market, ten minutes away from my home, and for forty years I've used this market. The colour and the street cries and the general assembly make this one of the most attractive markets in London. Number 12 bus from Big Ben, down the Walworth Road. Third stop is East Street, known locally as The Lane. Early closing Thursday at one.

K*

THE CALEDONIAN, in Bermondsey. Open Tuesdays and Fridays. The best day is Friday and the best time is between eleven and two. A bus to the Elephant and Castle, then another bus down Tower Bridge Road. A wonderful assortment of all manner of goods for sale, but don't expect to get Astounding Bargains. The sellers are mainly experts. Still, as I've said, even experts make mistakes. Has the best assembly of antiques to be found in any market in London.

BERWICK MARKET, off Shaftesbury Avenue. Number 12 bus to Piccadilly (going in the opposite way to East Street). Get off at Piccadilly Circus and walk for three minutes up Shaftesbury Avenue; second turning on the left is Rupert Street. Walk through the busy food and fruit market. At the top is a narrow alley which leads direct to Berwick Market. Sells everything. Has odd sellers of odd things. Best time to visit it is weekdays between noon and one-thirty.

FARRINGDON STREET. Nearest station Farringdon Street. A bus down
Holborn reaches this street. It is noted for its bookstalls, open every day,
but at its best around noon. It is not a big market, and if you are not
interested in books then it's not worth your time. In that case you will
be better served with the next market in the same area, which is Leather
Lane. Whereas Farringdon Street is open every day, I've never seen a
market of any consequence in Leather Lane on a Saturday.

DOUGLAS WAY, in Deptford. Nearest station, New Cross. Bus to the Elephant and Castle; then change on to a New Cross bus. It's a turning out of High Street, Deptford. It's at its best around noon on Saturdays— very colourful, with stalls selling just about everything from old clothes to odd gloves, from watches to ivory. It also sells flowers, fruit, and food. Many odd characters amongst both stall-holders and clients. A real working-class neighbourhood, nearly as good as East Street, Walworth.

PORTOBELLO ROAD, Notting Hill Gate. Go by Tube. It's open every day, but best between eleven and four on Saturdays. Entertaining characters, odd stalls selling everything from food to costly antiques. But, having been there on many occasions, I can assure you there are few if any bargains. Most of the stall-holders are experts and a good many of them display their wares at Caledonian Market on Fridays, so why see the same stuff on Saturdays? Still, it is one of the sights of London, with a great many coloured people in the crowds. Be careful here, for I've known of folks who had their pockets picked down the Portobello Road.

PETTICOAT LANE, Whitechapel. Go by Underground to Aldgate; then just follow the crowds. It's only on Sunday mornings, and at its best around eleven. A marvellous lot of traders, and a weird assortment of goods. Some of the traders even speak English! You can buy anything here; but do be careful.

DAWES STREET, Walworth. A curious small market: Sunday mornings only. Oddments of all sorts and sizes. Bikes of every age and make are something of a feature. (See my latest book, *The Last Bassoon*, for a fuller report on this and East Street markets.)

HIGH STREET, Battersea. Open every day, but best day Saturday. Mainly food with some odd stalls here and there. Battersea is a long way from Big Ben, but don't forget Battersea Park when in this area. Nice place to rest your tired feet in.

LEATHER LANE, Holborn. This is a market from Monday to Friday mainly for the use of city workers. It can be reached by Underground to Chancery Lane and then a short walk down the narrow turning beside Gamages. It's alive around noon and almost dead by two. Many bargains, and very good value, but not very colourful folks either behind or in front of the barrows. Sells everything, especially everything in metal, food, and household goods. A few antique stalls. No market on Saturdays or Sundays.

BRIXTON MARKET. Can be reached by bus from Big Ben. It's the heart of the coloured section of London, and when you walk this market you almost can think you are in Jamaica or Africa. Mainly it sells food and household goods. It also sells old clothes, and I've seen a stall there packed with second-hand gloves, thousands of them, mostly odd. Best day is Saturday and best time around two to five. No market on Sundays.

CLUB ROW, Bethnal Green. A curious Sunday-morning market mostly selling livestock, pets, birds, etc. I think this is a sad little place, perhaps because I love animals. Off Bethnal Green Road. Go by Underground.

LEWISHAM HIGH STREET. Open every day . . . but I think it's best Friday afternoons and Saturday mornings.

MILE END ROAD, Stepney. Go by Tube. The market takes place on what is called 'The Wastes', and only on Saturdays. It's almost like the Flea Market of Paris, with its odd junk stalls and odd characters. At its best around eleven. It will take about an hour to get there. It has nothing very rare or valuable. Caledonian Market has it all, only better, but it

[157]

must have its place in my list as a genuine open-air street market that is full of colour.

WARWICK WAY, off Vauxhall Bridge Road. A bus down Victoria Street and then a short walk. A small but gay market; many stall-holders are genuine 'cards'. Open every day, but Saturday afternoon is a good time. No market on Sundays.

STRUTTON GROUND, off Victoria Street. A short walk from Big Ben. Small and compact market, open every day: best time around one o'clock any day. Sells almost everything, but Berwick Market has it beaten for colour and that's why it's farther down the list. No market on Sundays.

RIDLEY ROAD, off Hackney High Street. A very long journey from Big Ben, as far as Lewisham in another direction. Genuine Cockney working-class market, but not a patch on East Street, and for that reason hardly worth the time and trouble to get there. At its best Fridays and Saturdays.

NORTHCOTE ROAD, Battersea. Off St John's Road; a long market, all manner of stalls, selling everything. Can be reached by bus. A working-class part of London. But Battersea High Street is a little better for local colour.

SOUTHWARK PARK ROAD. When you are at Caledonian Market you are within a mile of this market. Best day Saturday, say from eleven to four. Odd street cries and very good value in food.

TOWER BRIDGE ROAD, Bermondsey. A small part of the larger Caledonian Market. Open every day. Genuine Cockney stall-holders. I stood in this market myself for many years with my barrow of books.

BETHNAL GREEN ROAD. Open every day: sells everything. Can be reached by Tube. Is a characteristic part of working-class London. Sclater Street, Cygnet Street, Columbia Road, Cheshire Street, and Buck Lane markets are all in the same district, and all open on Sunday mornings.

ERMINGTON STREET, Camberwell. A small market which was once a grand market. Number 12 bus from Big Ben: get off at Camberwell Green. Cockney stall-holders, and mostly food. Saturdays up till two is its best time, but don't make a special journey.

CHAPEL STREET, Finsbury. A small and picturesque market, close to Angel Tube Station. Best day is Saturdays, around one to three.

LONDON FIELDS, Hackney. An odd collection of stalls. Open every day. A long journey from Big Ben, but it has some engaging stall-holders, and odd-looking customers.

LAMBETH WALK, Lambeth. A short walk over Westminster Bridge will get you to Lambeth Walk in fifteen minutes. Once a very famous market, the heart of Cockneyland. Strange cries still rise from the few stall-holders remaining there, but it is dying. The district is fast being rebuilt owing to bombing, and it is losing its character.

GREEMAN STREET, Islington. Open every day. A long journey, and 'The Wastes' at Mile End Road is better, but the customers make this an interesting place. Go by Underground.

BURSLEM STREET, Stepney. A small food market mainly for Jewish folks. Not open Saturdays. Petticoat Lane has it beaten. Near Aldgate Station, by Tube.

BERESFORD SQUARE, Woolwich. Open every day. Nearest station is Woolwich Arsenal. Hardly worth the time or trouble to see unless you happen to be in the neighbourhood. Nothing here for the seeker of antiques.

BLANDFORD STREET, Marylebone. Another rather long journey to a market that is in no way exceptional . . . mainly food. Lower Marsh is better for a similar market—but the customers *are* different.

DRAYCOTT STREET, Chelsea. Off King's Road. Can be reached by Tube to Sloane Square. The market is small. The customers are more interesting than the stall-holders, for this is the home of the artist and the beatnik.

[159]

LAVENDER HILL, Clapham. A very small and colourful market. Can be reached by bus. Working-class area of London, rather off the beaten track.

WELL STREET, Hackney. A small collection of stalls, mostly food. The Bethnal Green area is better for similar stalls, but Well Street has a good cross-section of working-class Londoners.

WHITECROSS STREET. Nearest Underground station is Moorgate; then a short walk. A very old market; I've known it for over forty years. It's rather like Leather Lane, being a market for city workers. It sells everything; best time for a visit is around noon. By three it's dead, and all the stalls vanished. It's not far from Farringdon Street, Exmouth, and Leather Lane markets, and each one has a style of its own.

CHAPEL STREET, Marylebone. (Not to be confused with the market of the same name in Finsbury.) Nearest Tube is Edgware Road. A tight and bright and busy little market. There is another market of much the same character in Bell Street, just five minutes' walk away from Chapel Street. Of the two, Chapel Street is the best. Many breezy stall-holders here, at both markets.

SEATON PLACE, Euston. A small, pleasant market, mostly selling food, rather like Warwick Way. Near to Warren Street Tube Station.

CHARLTON STREET, close to St Pancras Station. Has about a hundred stalls and very colourful. If you are 'doing' Seaton Market, Charlton is but ten minutes' walk away. Mainly sells food.

GOLBOURNE ROAD, Notting Hill. When you are in Portobello Road you may like to continue into this market, which is at the end of the Portobello Road, on the right. It's a very odd market, and well worth attention for its strange assorted lot of stall-holders, and odd things on barrows. Not quite so good as Portobello, but should not be missed when you are in this area. Sells everything. Best on Saturdays up till around four o'clock.

QUEEN STREET, close to St Pancras Station. Miscellaneous collection of stalls, a small walk away from Charlton Street.

NILE STREET, Shoreditch. A working-class, gay, and lively market. Very mixed assortment of stalls and barrows. Nearest station is Old Street. It's an odd part of London, and right off the average tourist's track. Open every day, best time around ten, but dead on Thursdays after one.

TACHBROOK STREET, Westminster. Off Vauxhall Bridge Road, near to Warwick Way. A very small but varied market. Open every day, but best on Fridays and Saturdays in the mornings.

WILCOX ROAD. Turning off South Lambeth Road, or can be reached via Wandsworth Road. A picturesque market, rather like Lower Marsh. Best day Saturday, ten till two.

KING STREET. Close to Camden Town Tube Station. Not so brisk or colourful as either Lower Marsh or Wilcox Road. Working-class customers. Varied goods for sale.

CHRISP STREET, Poplar, E.14. This is an interesting example because it is situated and provided for in the Lansbury Project of new dwellings to replace slums of this area. It is a very busy market that completely fits the neighbourhood. Although it's rather a long way (go by Tube) to Poplar, this is a splendid market and in a part of London seldom seen by visitors.

RATHBONE STREET, Canning Town. In the borough of West Ham, a small market of genuine Cockney characters. Was once famous, but is getting less and less. No market on Mondays, and is dead by one on Thursdays.

THE BROADWAY, in Hackney. An impressive title for a not so impressive market. Has many entertaining stall-holders, but is not outstanding in its general set-up. Closed on Thursdays. Go by Tube.

KINGSLAND ROAD, also in Hackney. A long road with a wide variety of stalls and barrows. Best day is Saturday around noon. Not quite so busy as East Street, Walworth, but has its fair share of vocal stall-holders. Go by train to Dalston Junction. Closed down on Thursday afternoons. Some stalls sell antiques in Kingsland Road.

WHITEHORSE STREET, Stepney. (Don't confuse this with Whitecross Street.) It's a considerable distance from Big Ben, but in an area of London that is worth exploration. All manner of stalls, of miscellaneous variety and with many genial characters. Whilst in the area of Stepney, find Watney Street, with another variety of barrows, close by. Open every day, but best time is in the mornings.

MARMONT STREET, Peckham. Go by the same number 12 bus that takes you to East Street and Westmoreland Road. It's a small turning, with a cinema on the corner, out of Peckham High Street. This is a small market of old clothes and oddments that is open only on Thursday and Saturday mornings. It's at its best by eleven and most stall-holders have gone away by one. It's reputed that there are often bargains to be had in this little market.

QUEENS ROAD, Upton Park. Go by Underground. It's a long journey, and not a particularly good market for variety, but it certainly has colour. Should you be in West Ham don't miss it. This is another market reputed to have very good bargains.

ANGEL LANE, Stratford. Go by Underground. A genuine Cockney market; there are few angels here. It's mostly for food and household goods: very few stalls of miscellaneous character.

SHEPHERD'S BUSH. Number 12 bus going along Oxford Street and past Bayswater gets you to this bright little market in thirty minutes or so. Some may argue that it's not a *street* market, but although all the stalls are covered-in, you, the buyers, are out in the open; although the stall-holders and their goods are protected from the rain the clients can get wet. It's behind the B.B.C. Theatre, close beside the railway bridge. You can also get there by Underground. It's a brisk, busy market and you can hardly move in it on a Saturday afternoon. Its advantage is that they don't need tarpaulins when the rain comes down, and as long as you have a good raincoat it's one of the few that you can visit on a wet day. At Shepherd's Bush, no matter what the day (except Sundays), there is bustle and life and colour.

GARNHAM STREET, in N.16, the borough of Hackney. Kingsland Road, in the same borough, and Ridley Road, close by, are considerably better

markets with a great deal more variety. But it's one of those small markets you are likely to miss, and if you are a marketite this is probably a new one for your list.

CHATSWORTH ROAD, Hackney, in the London area of E.9. Small but very lively. See Well Street Market nearby on the same journey.

HOLLOWAY ROAD, Islington. A small market, on Saturdays only; runs from Madras Road to the corner of Liverpool Road. Has a small collection of bric-à-brac and oddments' stalls. Also has fruit, vegetable, and house-hold-goods stalls.

SCLATER STREET, close to Bethnal Green Road. Can be reached by Tube. A very lively Sunday-morning-only market, not so big as Petticoat Lane, but most certainly worth a visit. At its best around eleven. Many odd stalls, odd stall-holders, selling almost everything.

CYGNET STREET, a turning off Sclater Street and a continuation of the above market. Sunday mornings only. Very small, packed, and bustling. Wide variety of goods for sale.

COLUMBIA ROAD, Bethnal Green. Close to Shoreditch Railway Station, and about ten minutes' walk from the two above markets. Again a Sunday-morning market; all manner of stalls and very odd characters. Worth visiting.

CHESHIRE STREET, Bethnal Green. Another Sunday-morning market. Brisk and busy, but not so busy as Petticoat Lane. It's in the near region of the above three markets, and it's certainly worth the ten minutes or so walk from Sclater Street to Cheshire Street, although what they sell is for the most part the same. Many of the stall-holders are 'cards'. Arnold Bennett liked this market.

BRICK LANE SOUTH has a market every day of the week. It's a turning out of Bethnal Green Road. I personally think that Leather Lane and East Street are better markets for many reasons, but it's worth going down when you are visiting this area of London.

ROMAN ROAD, Bethnal Green. If you continue down Bethnal Green Road, crossing over Cambridge Heath Road, you are in Green Street,

[163]

and this in turn leads you directly to Roman Road. There is a small market every day of the week in Roman Road, but it's hardly worth the twenty minutes or so extra journey, for Bethnal Green Road itself has more than Roman Road can offer. No market here on Sundays, and is dead on Thursdays by one o'clock.

BLACKWOOD STREET, Walworth. Second turning on the right going down East Street from the Walworth Road. A small but extremely busy market on Sunday mornings only. Noted for its flowers and roots, but in fact sells almost everything. Get there around noon and you'll hardly be able to move for the crowds. Good hunting. Number 12 bus from Big Ben will get you to East Street within twenty minutes.

RAILWAY APPROACH, London Bridge. Nearly opposite Southwark Cathedral (and do make a point of visiting this fine cathedral while in the neighbourhood). Although it would be a very enjoyable walk from Big Ben along the Embankment to London Bridge, it's a very long way. The best method is by Number 12 bus to the Elephant and Castle; alight there and get a 35 bus to the foot of London Bridge. Railway Approach is a very lively market, mostly devoted to flowers, fruit, and vegetables. It seems to be busy every hour of every day, except Sundays. Nothing in this market for the antique seeker, but in the near neighbourhood are many literary shrines connected with Shakespeare, Chaucer, and Dickens. American visitors would find this area of London very interesting.

These seventy street markets do not quite exhaust the number that can be found with diligent seeking. I am aware of street markets in Balham and Tooting, and even farther on the outskirts of London, but you would gain nothing by going so far afield. There is something just a little different in each of those listed above.

Finally, some practical advice. Avoid taking a wallet or a small purse. Divide up your money so that it is in several pockets. Take a nice big shopping bag, and in it put an extra pair of easy walking shoes. You are going to do a good deal of walking touring seventy markets, and at times your feet will be killing you. Finally, don't ever forget your raincoat; it's sure to rain, and these are for the most part open street markets. I wish you many bargains and hundreds of happy hours.

Silent Witnesses

ITALIAN DRAWINGS BY LAURENCE SCARFE

AMONG a race of humanists with the gift of unashamed expression the human figure has always taken first place, and each generation of Italians has left an artistic record of its manifold aspirations—records of pride, weeping, and laughter. The peninsula is therefore by now so crowded with statues that if they were gathered together they would easily overspill the square of St Peter's. They form, indeed, a secondary population, of stone, wood, wax, and plaster, in such great numbers, and so remarkably lively, that the traveller need never lack companionship provided he is content with silent communion. It becomes clear, when each statue is considered in historical context, that these creatures were regarded as more than mere symbols—they were in fact embodiments of the reality of the imagination, and as such were imbued with a psychic life of their own which could live on when their creators, and the generations to whom they were new art, were gone. We have therefore an extremely potent record of dreams, especially of those romantic and playful dreams in gardens, from which so many major styles in the arts evolved. This small collection of drawings deals in particular with that most fecund period,

the Baroque, the first truly modern art. Not only are they personal reminders of wanderings from northern Italy to Sicily, but also a slight indication of the variety and wealth of the subject. Though these figures are often of lesser artistic merit, they fulfil their own purpose, and augment the sunshine while in holiday mood.

The Angel in the Cloister of the Frari,
Venice: mid-eighteenth century

Figures from the *Commedia Veneziana* of the eighteenth century. They are members of a race of stone revellers encountered in considerable numbers in gardens, among dark bushes on moonlit nights, in Venice and the Veneto.

The bronze equestrian statue of Cosimo I, by Gianbologna, 1595, in the Piazza Signoria, Florence, seen at an unusual moment during the erection of stands for a concert.

The 'Rape of Helen' in marble, in the dark depths of a grotto decorated with a cement landscape and floral trellis-work in fresco. The group, by De Rossi; the grotto by Buontalenti; erected in the Boboli Gardens, Florence, about 1560.

The Sacro Bosco, Bomarzo; a little-known garden in the heart of the country. From the chapel-mausoleum, in a field of flowers, the way leads down the slope to a glen populated by colossal statues carved *in situ* from the natural boulders. This drawing shows the Mouth of Hell—the door alone is seven feet high; inside there is room for Pluto's banquet; the eyes are windows. We are in an allegorical Underworld of melancholy figures; carved, as far as is known, about 1560.

The Tiburtine Sibyl of the Villa d'Este, Tivoli, sits in her plant-grown, man-made glen in matriarchal magnificence. From beneath her feet a cascade falls into the great Ovato Fountain below. The date is approximately 1550.

One of two dwarf guardians of the gateway of the Villa Palagonia, Bagheria, Sicily. These are but two of the scores of playful eighteenth-century grotesques still remaining, from a veritable mob long since disappeared—memorials, along with other curiosities, of the caustic wit of the eccentric Prince.

In the Piazza Pretoria, Palermo, is what must be the largest fountain group in Italy, of which this is a detail. Scores of naked statues counterchange with animals' heads. The Palermitans, to excuse themselves, call this the *Piazza Vergogna*, the Square of Shame, on account of the nudity, but have nevertheless enjoyed the exhibition since 1575.

The lichened Fountain of the Giants in the Villa Lante, Bagnaia, erected by
Cardinal Gambera about 1570. Upon the terraces above are the *giochi d'acqua*,
where unsuspecting visitors are taken by surprise and sprayed with water from
hidden jets.

Eighteenth-century statues of our Lord and St Anne, two of a number salvaged from the wreckage and stacked in a corner after a collapse of the roof of the *duomo* of Caserta Vecchia, near Naples. St Anne is in flowered silk and has real hair.

The Shrine of Santa Rosalia on the summit of Monte Pelegrino, Palermo. A
richly clad marble of the saint lounges in a jewelled robe of chased gold. A child
angel hovers with a golden lily. All is solid gold—the skull, the book, the strew
of roses and flowers. She lies under the altar table behind plate glass, floodlit by
an office lamp. Here come the crowds of pilgrims, to the spot where Santa Rosalia
had her ecstasy; to leave *ex voto* offerings for favours received—wax replicas of
diseased parts of the body, hanks of hair, or photographs. They soak their hand-
kerchiefs in water dripping from the cave and pray for further miracles.

Sicilian puppets three or four feet high; creatures now of fantasy, but preserving memories of the Crusades, the wars against the Moors, the love affairs of medieval heroes, and a world of giant monsters. The cycle of plays takes a whole year to perform and can still be seen in Palermo.

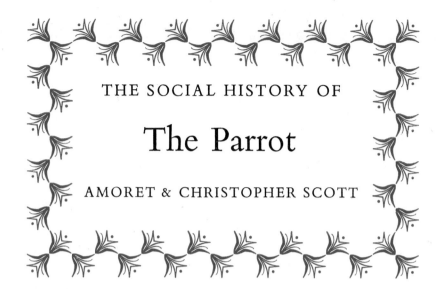

THE SOCIAL HISTORY OF

The Parrot

AMORET & CHRISTOPHER SCOTT

OVER fifteen million years ago, according to the evidence of Miocene fossils, there was a representative of the parrot family on the earth. But it had to wait for fourteen million years before there was a human voice for it to copy, and it spent the time perfecting its plumage and sharpening its vocal chords on the noises of the jungle. Parrots flourished in Africa and the Americas, on the islands sprinkled in the Pacific Ocean, in Asia and Australasia, and particularly in India. Only Europe was without parrots, and it was about 400 B.C. before it saw one.

Ctesias, a Greek doctor at the Persian Court, fired the imagination of Western civilization with his account of a bird which 'speaks the Indian language by nature and can be taught Greek', and soon afterwards one of Alexander the Great's captains brought some live specimens to Europe from the continent of India. It would seem that in spite of the many different members of the parrot family which existed there, only one kind was known to the Greeks and Romans. From the descriptions of Aristotle and later writers, it was probably what we now know as a Ringneck Parrakeet. Aristotle called the bird *psittake*, a word almost identical with the name given it in Ceylon, its probable source.

The Greeks, and after them the Romans, were delighted with the new acquisition from the East. Colourful, intelligent, and with this miraculous ability to imitate the human voice, the parrot was soon established in the Courts and in every rich household. Glimpses of the bird appear in writings throughout the course of the Roman Empire. Pliny tells us that

M

parrots which would not learn their lessons were punished by beatings with an iron rod. Ovid and Statius both wrote elegies on the death of favourite birds (the subject of Statius's lament lived in a cage with silver bars and decorations in tortoiseshell and ivory). Cato the Elder sourly prophesied that the Republic was doomed as long as its men carried parrots on their wrists; and that disgusting old glutton the Emperor Heliogabalus made a habit of serving parrots' heads at his banquets.

The collapse of the Roman Empire dropped a portcullis across the path of history, and the story of parrots, in common with many other subjects of almost equal importance, was suspended for a thousand years while the Dark Ages ran their course. It seems very likely that the warriors returning from the early Crusades should bring back with them some of the parrots which are native to Asia Minor, and which must have been kept as amusing pets by the Arabs. But the first tangible record we have of the parrot after the collapse of Rome is in the World Map at Hereford Cathedral, a fascinating representation of the then known world in its orthodox flat form. The World Map was drawn as a means of mass instruction in about 1300, and represents the bird as a native of India in accordance with Roman descriptions. It is obvious that no new information on the parrot family had become available since the power of Rome had ended, and that the artist had drawn on largely Roman authors for his material.

The medieval Bestiaries, popular accounts of animals derived from one source (Physiologus—'the Naturalist') in the late Roman Empire, merely retail Pliny's advice as to beating a parrot with an iron bar and give little other helpful information. Solinus (second century), however, as translated by Golding in 1587, advanced our knowledge of parrot characteristics by declaring that a well-bred and potentially voluble bird had five toes to each foot, as opposed to the silent, stupid, ill-bred three-toed variety. The value of this information to the naturalist is lessened by the knowledge that all the *Psittacidae* have four toes to each foot.

A parrot is shown as part of the congregation in a thirteenth-century illuminated manuscript devoted to the life of St Francis of Assisi. Chaucer's fourteenth-century England knew parrots well (they could 'cry "Wat!", as well as can the Pope'), and called them 'popinjays' or 'papingoes'; the name was a corruption of the Arabic 'Baboghai', as a result of the influx of Arab traders to Venice, the centre of the Renaissance world. The little parrakeet was apparently still the only parrot known

[178]

to Europe, for the term 'popinjay' was used in the sixteenth century to describe the shade of electric green characteristic of the Ringneck.

It was at this time that the African Grey parrot, the most intelligent and the most accomplished talker of the whole tribe, made its appearance in the Western world. One of the first to arrive was sold to a Venetian cardinal for the unprecedented sum of one hundred gold pieces; it should be added that the cunning Arab who made the sale had already taught the bird to repeat the Pater Noster and the Credo—no mean achievement.

The Renaissance brought the trappings of luxury to all the Courts of Europe, and parrots became an essential part of the train of every lady of fashion—as indispensable as dwarfs and monkeys and fools. Their cages were provided with mirrors for their amusement, and the floors covered daily with fresh flowers. We are indebted to John Skelton (1460–1529) for the following description of a fifteenth-century Ringneck parrakeet:

> With my becke bent, my lyttyl wanton eye,
> My fedders freshe as is the emrawde green,
> About my neck a cyrculet lyke the ryche rubye,
> My lyttyll leggys, my feet both fete and clene,
> I am a mynon to wayt uppon a quene;
> My proper Parrot, my lyttyl pretty foole,
> With ladyes I lerne, and go with them to scole.

Columbus's discovery of the American continent in 1492 caused a revolution in the ranks of the medieval parrot-fanciers. The diminutive *Santa Maria* returned from its historic journey bearing not only eye-witness accounts of the wonders of the South American jungles, but some live macaws to boot—birds which made the familiar parrakeet and the recently introduced African Grey look like poor relations. The gathering of the new continents to the rapacious breasts of European traders and adventurers resulted in a regular but well-controlled supply of rare parrot-like birds flowing into England by the late sixteenth century—'loories' and 'perroquets' and macaws (the latter, a purely South American bird, inexplicably named after the Portuguese colony of Macao on the coast of China). The judicious control of the import trade kept up the price and so ensured that only the most worthy of the great ones should have the privilege of exhibiting such rarities; the possession of a macaw was virtually restricted to members of the Royal Family (although, morals being what they were, this was a comparatively wide group).

[179]

Both King Henry VIII and his Chancellor, Sir Thomas More, were parrot-fanciers; the latter, in fact, customarily had at least a dozen flying freely round his house. Literature of the Elizabethan age abounds with references—a good half-dozen can be found in Shakespeare's plays alone, most of them metaphorical ('Drunk? and speak parrot? and squabble? swagger? swear? and discourse fustian with one's own shadow?'—*Othello*, II, 3). Shakespeare was no doubt familiar at first hand with the macaws and parrots of his patrons, but to the great majority of his audiences they were still only slightly less fabulous than the basilisk and the phoenix (both creatures firmly believed in and actually *seen* by a friend of a friend who had a cousin in the *Golden Hind*).

Some time in the middle years of the seventeenth century the first cockatoo arrived in this country; this is substantiated by a portrait, painted by Simon Verelst in about 1650, of Anne Russell, a daughter of the subsequent first Duke of Bedford, holding a Sulphur Crested Cockatoo. The date is interesting, for Australia was not officially discovered until 1770. This exclusively Australasian bird must therefore have been picked up by one of the navigators who cruised in those unknown waters early in the seventeenth century, and who probably set foot on the new continent without realizing his discovery.

King Charles II was the most prominent bird-fancier of his day, and he has left to posterity the name, if not the appurtenances, of Birdcage Walk, which was bounded on each side by enclosed aviaries filled with rare and beautiful birds. The King's favourite mistress, the Duchess of Richmond and Lennox, kept for forty years an African Grey parrot to which she was devoted. When 'La Belle Stuart' died (in 1702) she left detailed instructions in her will for the making of a wax effigy of herself to be dressed in the robes she had worn at the coronation of Queen Anne. Her beloved parrot survived her by only a few days, and although not mentioned in her will, was stuffed and placed on a bracket beside her, where it still stands in the Undercroft of Westminster Abbey—the oldest stuffed bird in Britain.

The snob-value of owning a macaw was enormous. The socially established and, in particular, the socially aspiring went to the greatest trouble to ensure not only that they had a macaw, but that everyone was thoroughly acquainted with the fact. Leading painters (notably Bogdani and several painters of the Dutch School in the latter part of the seventeenth century, and Reynolds in the eighteenth century) did a roaring

[180]

Anne Russell, daughter of the first Duke of Bedford, painted by Simon Verelst (*c.* 1637–1710). In the collection at Woburn; reproduced by courtesy of the Duke of Bedford. The presence of the Sulphur Crested Cockatoo in the painting is remarkable, for Australia was not officially discovered until 1770; the cockatoo is found nowhere else but on the Australian continent.

Above is a White Cockatoo, with other birds, painted by the Dutch artist Jan Weenix (1640–1719). On the opposite page is a detail from a large still life by Jan Fyt (1611–1661), a painter of the Flemish School, showing a page holding up a bunch of grapes to an excellently painted African Grey. (Both pictures in the Wallace Collection.)

The Blue and Yellow Macaw, one of the finest of Edward
Lear's illustrations in his *Family of Psittacidae or Parrots*
published in 1830–2.

Leadbeater's Cockatoo, from John Gould's *Birds of Australia*. Gould, an expert, regarded this bird as 'the most beautiful and elegant of the genus yet discovered'.

Examples of the parrot *motif* in very different art forms. The gold and jewelled pendant above, on the right, is Spanish and was made in the sixteenth century (Victoria and Albert Museum). The two song covers are delightful examples of lithographic work of the mid-Victorian period. The high incidence of parrot themes in the popular music of this time is proof of the social popularity of the parrot in the Victorian drawing-room.

Another mid-Victorian song cover, depicting a cockatoo of some sort.

[187]

A painting by Jan Davidsz de Heem (c. 1600–c. 1683), of an African Grey and a Blue-fronted Amazon parrot. Reproduced by courtesy of the Leonard Koetser Gallery.

trade in studies and family groups which included a macaw. Sir Joshua, in fact, kept a macaw as a prominent member of his own household and it was used as a prop in several of his canvases. The story is told that James Northcote, as a pupil of Reynolds, painted a portrait of the servant girl whose duties included clearing up after the macaw. Relations between girl and bird were obviously strained, for when the completed canvas was brought into the macaw's view for the first time, it launched itself across the room and did its best to tear the portrait to pieces. Northcote rightly regarded this as a compliment.

One of the most engaging of the eccentric characters of the eighteenth century was Colonel Dennis O'Kelly, born poor in Ireland in about 1720, a sedan-chair man, gigolo, billiard-marker in London, and then owner of the celebrated race-horse Eclipse. The profits which he made from the possession of this remarkable horse (and an equally remarkable skill at cards) elevated his social position with some rapidity, and he became the possessor of a colonelcy in the Middlesex Regiment, a fine estate at Cannons, and a parrot that was almost as famous as was Eclipse. The following extract is taken from a newspaper report of 1822:

> A few days ago, died, in Half Moon Street, Piccadilly, the celebrated Parrot of Colonel O'Kelly. This singular bird sang a number of songs, in perfect time and tune. She could express her wants articulately, and give her orders in a manner nearly approaching rationality. Her age was not known. It was, however, more than thirty years; for previous to that period, Colonel O'Kelly bought her, at Bristol, for one hundred guineas. The Colonel was repeatedly offered five hundred guineas-a-year for the bird, by persons who wished to make a public exhibition of her; but this, out of tenderness to the favourite, he constantly refused. This bird could not only repeat a great number of sentences, but also answer a number of questions put to her. When she sung, she beat time, with all the regularity of a scientific performer; and she seemed so much alive to musical melody, that, if she mistook a note by accident, she would again revert to the bar where she had committed the error, still, however, waiting time, and finishing her song, with much accuracy.

Parrot concerts were held at the house in Half Moon Street, and on these occasions it is reported that the street was quite blocked with carriages.

The nineteenth century saw a great change in the position of the parrot family in society and in science. The Industrial Revolution caused a re-distribution of wealth and a consequent multiplication of the rungs on

[189]

the social ladder; parrots ceased to be the prerogative of the rich and became symbols of the new middle-class respectability (hence the spate of Victorian jokes about parrots/sailors/bad language/shocked visitors). No over-furnished Victorian drawing-room was complete without its parrot (usually a green Amazon or an African Grey) in its heavy brass cage complete with green-baize cover. Then, as now, they were not everyone's idea of all that is amusing and desirable: Jane Carlyle in a letter to her mother in 1839 wrote: 'Some new neighbours, that came a month or two ago, brought with them an accumulation of all the things to be guarded against in a London neighbourhood, viz. a pianoforte, a lap-dog, and a parrot.'

The moneyed aristocracy of the nineteenth century assisted scientific study of exotic birds by establishing large private aviaries ; prominent among these noble naturalists were the Earl of Derby, Lord Lilford, and the twelfth Duke of Bedford. The first quarter of the century, in particular, was an age of geographical and zoological curiosity, and scarcely a year went by without a new colony being added to the Empire and a new bird to human knowledge. It was, in fact, the first time in history that a serious attempt had been made to classify the birds and beasts of the world in a truly scientific manner; it took the whole of the century, and a good deal of the next, to tie up the loose ends.

Furious squabbles were continually breaking out among authorities on the *Psittacidae* as to whether newly discovered birds (a large number of which were named after their finders—Barnard's Parrakeet, Swainson's Lorikeet, Banksian Cockatoo, Levaillant's Amazon, and so on) were in fact new *genera* or only *sub-genera* of a known *genus*, and many pages of the scientific journals were covered with learned arguments.

Even more difficult was the unwrapping of the sentimentality with which even the most dedicated of nineteenth-century naturalists would insist on covering their life's work. The following extract from *The Speaking Parrots* by Dr Karl Russ, a noted Victorian authority on birds, will illustrate this: 'If an animal be able, though only partially, to imitate human language, it must decidedly belong to higher ranks of creation even than those which appear most to resemble man.' This grossly misleading conclusion from an eminent ornithologist was written as late as 1894. Other Victorian naturalists persisted in maintaining that the sole purpose of the bright colours of the parrot family's plumage was to give pleasure to the human eye; it was some time before a more objective

comparison was made with similar defensive colour schemes in the animal kingdom (such as that of the wasp).

Nevertheless, enormous ornithological progress was made throughout Victoria's long reign. A few names stand out in the chronicles of parrot history: William Swainson (1789–1855), a zoologist draughtsman who taught himself lithography in order to illustrate his researches; Edward Stanley, thirteenth Earl of Derby (1775–1851), a devoted naturalist whose private menagerie occupied a hundred acres of land and seventy of water —areas kept stocked by agents all over the world (the Derbyan Parrakeet and Stanley Parrakeet are both named after him); and perhaps the most important of all, Edward Lear.

Lear, to most people, means Nonsense Rhymes and limericks, but his fame should rest on more substantial foundations than these. Born in 1812, the last of a family of twenty-one children, entirely self-taught as an artist, painter, and lithographer, he produced a series of lithographed illustrations of the members of the parrot tribe (*The Family of Psittacidae or Parrots*, published 1830–2) which have never been surpassed.

Lear was drawing, and earning money for it, by the time he was fifteen. When he was eighteen he obtained permission to make drawings of parrots at the newly opened Gardens of the Zoological Society, and used the studies for the illustrations to his work—drawn and lithographed by himself at the age of twenty. The illustrations were recognized, by artists and ornithologists alike, as being in a class by themselves both for accuracy and for naturalness. After exhausting the resources of the Zoological Society he enlarged his sphere of operations to draw from birds in the collections of the Earl of Derby (then Lord Stanley) at Knowsley Hall, and others, and, as a last resort, from stuffed birds lent by John Gould, the taxidermist to the Zoological Society.

Gould was an odd and unlikeable character. Lear's talent was obvious, and a revelation to him, and he used the struggling young artist for his own ends in a most unscrupulous manner. Gould's published works, in fact, notably *Birds of Europe*, 1832–7, depended very largely upon his wife's skill as a lithographer and Lear's (and later William Hard's) as an artist.

By the end of the nineteenth century some four hundred members of the parrot family had been classified; the family (*Psittacidae*) was divided into sub-families (*Loriinae*, including lories and lorikeets; *Kakatoeinae*, the cockatoos—the name is clearly imitative of the bird's voice; *Psittacinae*,

including macaws, parrots, and parrakeets—to name the principal ones), and each *genus* in the sub-family was named with scientific accuracy. As all these birds are frequently seen in captivity all over the world, the rule of thumb advises that cockatoos all have crests and come from Australasia; lories have tongues specially adapted to extract nectar from flowers; lorikeets are the same with long tails; macaws are the biggest of the lot and have bare skin round the eyes; parakeets are parrots with long tails.

There were, and still are, a number of popular misconceptions about members of the parrot family. The most prevalent was that they survive for anything up to a hundred and fifty years, and are therefore handed down from generation to generation as they outlive their owners. An engaging story on this aspect of the parrot is that of the early-nineteenth-century explorer Humboldt, who is said to have discovered in South America an aged parrot teaching the astonished natives the language of the Atures, a race long since vanished from the earth. The *Guiness Book of Records* says that the oldest *proven* case is that of a cockatoo aged ninety-five; the usual life-span of the larger parrot-like birds is thirty to forty years.

The other gross misconception, and one which appears to have a surprising hold on the imagination, is that it is necessary for the tongue of a bird to be split before it can talk. This is an extraordinary medieval survival, and it cannot be emphasized too strongly that nothing of the kind is necessary. Some *genera* of the parrot family will learn to imitate human speech much more quickly than others; some never will.

Although the Victorian era is usually regarded as the golden age of the parrot, there are many more parrots in England today than at any time in history. A surprising statement? The budgerigar (more accurately the Undulating Grass Parrakeet) is the sole pet in an enormous number of homes. Though small, it can be an accomplished talker. Of course, the budgerigar cannot compare with the Victorian conception of a parrot—big enough to be a piece of furniture, long-lived, practically human in intelligence—but it is nevertheless an unfailing source of pride and amusement.

La Vie Bohème

BY TUDOR EDWARDS

THERE IS indeed nothing new under the sun. The Beatniks of today are no doubt convinced that their revolt against society is without precedent, and that they carry the badge of their defiance with an air of *panache* hitherto unknown. Angry young men and Chelsea Set women, impatient for recognition of their talents, suffering from the spiv mentality that shies away from a routine job of work, and conscious of the transience and uncertainty of life in an atomic world, seem blissfully unaware that earlier generations reacted in much the same way.

Certainly the outward manifestations have changed. The Welfare State has provided rebels with some measure of economic security, the duffel-coat or Edwardian suit are within the reach of all. The young women are braver, for they stifle their figures where their predecessors flaunted them, save for that minority that now affects the short gym-dresses of *Lolita*.

There are, however, more essential differences, differences of morality and belief. The Beatniks, born into a culture based on jazz and technology, lack the unique Continental state of mind and the single-mindedness of purpose of their prototypes. The classic Bohemian survived without State aids, his preoccupation with Art was absolute, and he had a greater capacity for pleasure—and martyrdom. He was, in fact, cast in more heroic mould.

To most people *la vie Bohème* means the Moulin Rouge and Toulouse-Lautrec—and an opera by Puccini in which someone's tiny hand is frozen.

Now this is not meant to be funny; it is, in fact, an indication of how a musician of stature, if not genius, can wholly misinterpret and deform what is, within its own special limits, a true work of art. For *La Bohème* is based upon Henri Murger's *Scènes de la vie de Bohème*. So is Leoncavallo's rival opera of the same name, produced a year later, and thus handicapped, to Leoncavallo's chagrin, for it was he who put the idea into Puccini's head. Aptly enough, Puccini wrote most of the opera in the Bohème Club at Torre del Lago near Milan. From a dramatic point of view the opera is eminently successful, and it is a guaranteed tearjerker. Debussy, of all people, could say that he knew of no one who had described the Paris of that time as well as Puccini in *La Bohème*. One can only insist that none of this is Murger.

Henri Murger was born into a Paris of political flux and turmoil, of a mother who shortly afterwards left him for the grave and a father who worked as a *concierge* and did odd-job tailoring, having been a regimental tailor in the *grande armée* of Napoleon. His unambitious father's plans to cast the son in the same mould were foiled, for young Henri had a head filled with poetry and painting and he became a dreaming lawyer's clerk. After the death of the mother the two males were constantly at loggerheads, until Murger *père* threw the younger man out. Henri joined his friend Lilioux in a miserable garret in the Rue Montsigny. The renegade bourgeois, the embryo man of letters, cocked a snook at the rest of the world, and for a few years nothing was heard of him.

His mode of life and activities were revealed in the short stories that began to appear from 1845 in *Le Corsaire*, the little review which published poems by Baudelaire and which petered out during the Second Empire. He was then twenty-three (he was to live only sixteen years more), and it was soon clear that the sketches and burlesque narratives of life in the Latin Quarter were based on that led by himself and his friends. They were so popular that in November of 1849 a dramatic adaptation, *La Vie de Bohème*, was given at the Variétés, and when two years later the stories appeared in book form he was the literary lion of the capital. He wrote other books, among them *Le Pays Latin*, *Les Buveurs d'eau*, and *Le Sabot rouge*, usually variations on the same theme, but never again did he achieve such a *tour de force* as his first book.

Bohemia was a by-product of the Revolution and its radical if topsy-turvy changing of the social order, and of the spirit of revolt still rampaging through Europe. It could exist anywhere where young writers,

painters, sculptors, and musicians were trying to express themselves in the face of poverty and bourgeois apathy. The Bohemian was a sort of anarchist, renouncing the values and conventions of society, renouncing black coats and drawing-rooms. He lived from day to day, in a squalor that was accidental and not of his own choosing—indeed he was basically a fastidious soul—and his façade of gay mockery often concealed inward cries of despair. His morals were no worse than those of a prosperous business man or even of a member of the Institut de France; it was merely that he displayed them, or the lack of them, more blatantly. All he suffered was endured in the name of Art. His slogan, as Gautier phrased it a little later, was *L'Art pour l'Art*, or Art for Art's sake. Bohemia became a cult.

In Paris the Bohemia of the 'forties meant the *Quartier latin*, the university quarter on the Left Bank, so called because in the Middle Ages the common tongue of the students from all over the world was Latin, which gradually came to be identified with the arts. It covered roughly the area from the Seine to the Montagne Sainte-Geneviève, and from the Rue du Bac on the west to the Rue Cardinal-Lemoine on the east. It was dominated then, as now, by the dome of Soufflot's Panthéon. The Boulevard Saint-Michel had not yet been cut, and the quarter was a warren of ancient buildings peopled with every type from aristocrat to rag-picker.

Into this loosely knitted fraternity of saints and sinners Murger dived to spend the rest of his short life, and from it he created Rodolphe and Mimi, Marcel and Musette, Schaunard and Phémie, not forgetting Colline, the philosopher, and Uncle Monetti, the stove merchant who excels in relating the retreat from Moscow. Rodolphe is a poet by inclination but a hack-writer by compulsion. Marcel is a painter whose masterpiece, 'The Crossing of the Red Sea', is obviously intended for the Louvre but will finish up as a grocer's shop-sign. Schaunard is a musician, planning the great symphony (which, of course, he will never complete), 'The Influence of Blue on the Arts'.

Here is a clique of merry paupers with talents paralysed, surely, by poverty, competition, and the greedy, crafty, Philistine bourgeois. Yet what roistering fellows they are, eating whenever they can, making love whenever they can, continuously selling, pawning, and borrowing— Rodolphe especially sponging (in the nicest way, of course) on his Uncle Monetti—and always hard-pressed to find a decent coat or hat or shoes for an evening out.

Their respective lodgings—when they contrive to remain in them by

playing scurvy tricks on their long-suffering landlords, who have scarcely seen a sou in rent—are in dim, dingy garrets, and they are for ever retreating skywards to higher and cheaper rooms. Furniture is a luxury one dispenses with. A bed, of course, a chair, perhaps a table, perhaps an easel. As like as not most of the furniture is sawn up to feed the stove in a desperate effort to stave off the polar wind hurtling through the windows. It could possibly disappear in other ways. In the Bohemia of a few years later Whistler, the painter, greeted the American friend who had brought the long-overdue remittance with 'I've just eaten my washstand.' To make up for the bareness of the rooms, artists would create an illusion by drawing furniture on the bare, white walls.

There are times, of course, when one is locked out and without the necessary trifle for a night's lodging. One might then find oneself, like Rodolphe, 'on the Avenue de Saint-Cloud, in the third tree on the left as you leave the Bois de Boulogne, on the fifth branch'.

And the women, oh, the women! Mimi, Musette, and Phémie are or were *grisettes*, 'those pretty girls who were a mixture of the bee and the grasshopper, who sang at their work all the week long, never asked anything of God but a little sunshine on Sundays. They loved with their hearts, in their vulgar fashion, and sometimes threw themselves out of windows.' They are also completely devoid of moral sense and have prodigious records of promiscuity: that they should be faithful to one man is quite preposterous. They are illiterate and cannot spell, but, as Marcel puts it, 'White arms and shoulders have no need of grammar.' When all three couples set up house in barely furnished rooms in a block in the once fashionable Faubourg Saint-Germain the other tenants sleep on a volcano and at the end of the month unanimously give the landlord notice. This *ménage* cannot last. After six months the epidemic of divorce breaks out. It begins when Schaunard's aesthetic sense is offended by the discovery that one of Phémie's knees is inferior to the other, so he dismisses her. Within a few weeks Mimi and Musette, tired of poverty, have found aristocratic 'protectors'.

In Bohemia indeed everything was transitory, everything except the search for sensation, the delight in beauty, and the game of love. The partner might change, but the game went on. Love was aspiration, the unknown, delusion, and was not to be confused with the bourgeois institution of marriage, with its shackles and responsibility. So systematically were love adventures conducted that Murger's contemporary, Gavarni,

[196]

the artist, could head that particular section of his journal: 'Classification of Butterflies'. Rodolphe keeps the letters and souvenirs of his mistresses in a drawer he calls 'the catacombs of love'.

So the comedy of disorder and revolt goes on, and the odd francs are always found by one device or another. Rodolphe writes a 'medico-chirurgico-odontological poem' for a celebrated dentist and an epitaph for a tombstone. Marcel paints portraits of grenadiers at the Ave-Maria barracks—eighteen sitters at six francs each. Schaunard plays discordant scales on a piano from early morning until late evening, every day for a fortnight, in the rooms and on the instruction of an Englishman, simply to annoy an actress on the floor below whose parrot keeps the English-man awake at night. This combined fortune takes the three Bohemians, with Mimi, Musette, and Phémie, who have returned to the fold (only to fly off again shortly), on a spree into the countryside. Money, after all, is useful only for feasting and dressing the women. There is little enough opportunity for either, and eating is a problem. Lent invariably lasts far longer than it should. One goes to one's worst enemy's if a good meal is to be had. After a long period of abstinence Rodolphe and Mimi give a dinner (with crockery!), and Colline cruelly refuses to exchange his portion of tipsy-cake for a ticket of admission to the orangery at Versailles offered him by Schaunard.

For preference, of course, they dine out. They go, probably, to Mère Cadet's in the Chaussée du Maine, celebrated for its rabbit-stew and *choucroute*, the venue of carters, women singers from Montparnasse, variety artistes from the Bobino music-hall, and literary amateurs. Certainly they eat, drink, and play dominoes in the Café Momus in the Rue des Prêtres Saint-Germain l'Auxerrois, on the Right Bank and near the Louvre, and they eat at the Provençal restaurant in the Rue Dauphiné, noted for its *aïolli* and its literary waiters. Their fellows knew the smoke-hazy Dinochau, a little cabaret in the Rue Bréda, and the Café Soufflet on what is now the Boulevard Saint Michel, which in 1934 became the Dupont-Latin, with a new décor for a new generation of artists and students. They would certainly have known Chez Flicoteaux in the Place Sorbonne, which closed in 1848. There, a homely dinner of three dishes and a carafe of wine was served for eighteen sous in what Balzac described as 'a workshop and not a festival hall'.

When the Bohemians were particularly flush and could borrow coats, hats, and shoes they would cross to the Right Bank, to the Café de la

[197]

Régence near the Palais Royal, which Rodolphe calls Providence Square, for one was sure to meet creditors there. The restaurant still stands, enlarged and altered. Founded early in the eighteenth century, it had a celebrated chess-room where would be found Europe's greatest chess-players. In the 'forties Henri Murger himself, with Théophile Gautier, Gerard de Nerval, Alfred de Musset, and other picaresque characters, would often be seen sitting beneath the wonderful mirrors. At every first night of the Théâtre-Français, Barbey d'Aurevilly, the dandy, came here for a slice of ham and a kirsch—in waisted frock-coat and white trousers with velvet piping, vast shirt-frill, gauntlet gloves, and ample cloak lined with purple silk. This was an heroic age. Gautier wore a scarlet doublet. Nerval, who popularized midnight onion soup at Les Halles, used to saunter along the streets leading a lobster on a blue ribbon; he squandered his fortune in an orgy of walking-sticks and a debauch of opera-glasses, and then hanged himself from a lamp-post outside a tramps' doss-house that had refused him a night's lodging.

Outside the Quarter proper the favourite resort of the Bohemians at this time was probably the Brasserie des Martyrs, up the steep hill that leads past the church of Notre-Dame de Lorette to Montmartre, though Montmartre was then a village and the Place du Tertre the village square. Here would be found all the *ratés*, the seedy, middle-aged failures of Bohemia, the wild, bearded *rapins*, or 'daubers', as the artist-students were called, and their equally wild women, including many a Mimi who, unromantically, had failed to die young. Lording it over them sat Baudelaire, 'the hermit of the brothel', whose *Les Fleurs du Mal* had only just scandalized Paris, and Henri Murger, a spectral figure with bloodshot eyes and ragged beard, reading, perhaps, the *Chanson de Musette*, his best poem.

Occasionally the famous courtesans drifted into these places, dressed out of *Le Moniteur de la Mode* and *Le Petit Courrier des Dames*, the fashion journals akin to the more obscure *The Scarf of Iris* that Rodolphe professed to edit, though when and where is never made quite clear. This was the age of Gavarni and Constantine Guys, in whose drawings indeed Rodolphe and Mimi and their friends may be seen.

Then there were the little bistros where they dropped in at night, at the 'green hour', the hour of absinthe. Near the Seine there were rustic farmhouse-like restaurants, where the men could drink and play cards in summer-houses or stand at the bowling alley in the garden. There were the *bals populaires*, the dance-halls or places of amusement that catered for

every class. Notable among these was the Bal Bullier, which formed part of the Closerie des Lilas, a café on the Boulevard Montparnasse, where lights hung in the trees and the girls danced with a drunken viscount or a pomaded drayman. The Can-Can was still fairly new, intoxicating, and scandalous, not yet the innocent dance of Offenbach. It was first danced in Paris in 1831 at a low tavern, was said to have been brought over from Algeria, and was introduced to the public a year later at the annual carnival at the Variétés, when the police tried to break it up. Another infamous dance, though then known only to a few, was Musard's *Galop Infernal*, first danced at the devilish parties held by Petrus Borel in the Rue d'Enfer, where ice-cream was served in skulls.

Paris was still a medieval city, the labyrinth of sinister, narrow, cobbled streets described by Victor Hugo and Eugene Sue, and the flaring gaslamps had not long replaced oil lanterns. There were street brawls and riots, and barricades of upturned carts, chairs, and mattresses would be hastily thrown up to keep police and soldiers back. Not yet had Haussmann cut the city into squares and segments and unrolled his great boulevards.

Mimi's downfall lay not in going to live with Rodolphe but in leaving him for others, just as a courtesan fell when she gave her favours freely. She had to die young and of consumption, for we are here at the tail-end of the Romantic epoch, and indeed the death of Mimi is paralleled in *La Dame aux Camélias*, the Dumas romance published in 1848. At the end Mimi is one with Manon Lescaut, Marguerite Gautier (The Lady of the Camelias), Madame Bovary, and Louise.

The story of Francine and Jacques that enters briefly into Murger's book is an isolated self-contained story that has no valid place in the narrative and the sequence of events, and Murger could have introduced it only as a dramatic element that would instil a sense of premonition in the reader. This gave Puccini his chance, and in the interests of box-office he twisted the story so that Mimi lies on her death-bed in Rodolphe's garret and begs for a muff because her hands are cold. She thrusts her hands into it with a sigh of pleasure, sinks back and dies. 'Oh, my youth,' cries Rodolphe, 'it is buried with you!' Had Puccini leavened his sticky sentiment and gloom with something of the hilarious spirit of Strauss's *Die Fledermaus* he would have been nearer the mark, and would have saved Murger's book from near-extinction.

[199]

But who was the real Mimi? Was she an amalgam of Rodolphe's four mistresses, Louise, Laure, Lucille, Juliette—a compound, in fact, of Murger's four mistresses? For they had their counterparts in real life. The first was the blonde, cerulean-eyed wife of a notary turned criminal. The second was another flaxen-haired minx who, after a tiff with Murger following a Christmas party at which she got drunk, walked out on him, only to return, like the legendary Mimi, starving, contrite, and mortally tubercular. The third golden-haired beauty held out promise of domestic bliss and was level-headed enough in the kitchen. The fourth post-dated the *Le Corsaire* stories. Nearer than the others in intellect to Murger, her brunette vivacity caused him to coax her out of her flat and into his, a move that meant merely crossing the road, for they lived opposite each other in the Rue Notre-Dame de Lorette. There they lived happily together until Murger's death ten years later, his physical and mental powers exhausted at the age of thirty-nine.

The tragedy of Bohemia lay in the endless failures, the ultimate disillusion. Ardent and carefree youth lived from day to day, until it woke up one morning to find itself middle-aged, with nothing achieved and no future. Murger himself and perhaps one or two of his companions were more fortunate. When the *Scènes* end, Rodolphe has written a successful book, Marcel has broken into the *Salon*, and Schaunard's songs are being sung at all the concerts. Murger end on a cynical note, but the bravado and make-believe have gone. As Marcel says: 'I've no objection to contemplating the past; but it must be through a bottle of real wine, and sitting in a comfortable chair. There's nothing to be done about it—I'm corrupt: nowadays I like only the good things of life!' Gautier used to say defiantly that if he had an income of twelve hundred francs a year he would retire to the Latin Quarter and live the life of a student and work a lifetime on a volume of sonnets. His income was a splendid one, and he did not retire to the Quarter.

By the time that Alphonse Daudet arrived in the Latin Quarter in the 'fifties Bohemianism had changed, had become more viciously decadent, as Daudet makes clear in his *Trente Ans de Paris*. George du Maurier was there at the same time, though as an English gentleman he was rarely in the scrum, and by the time he wrote his celebrated novel of Bohemia, *Trilby*, Anglo-Saxon convention had so coloured his mind that, despite Trilby, the model who sits for the altogether, his exiles suggest the Chelsea Arts Ball. There is a suggestion in both Daudet and du Maurier,

however, that Murger may have seen the Quarter through rose-coloured spectacles.

Many factors hastened the decline of Bohemia. Under the Second Empire there arose a new irregular section of society, *le demi-monde*, which largely superseded Bohemia as its *cocottes* came to supersede the Mimis and Musettes of the garrets. Then came the physical transformation of Paris under the architect-planner Haussmann, creating a luxury city on the west and drawing many wealthy people away from districts like the Marais, the Faubourg Saint-Antoine, and the entire Latin Quarter, where formerly the social classes, rich and poor, were thrown together, and where much of the characteristic huddle of historic if slummy buildings was now demolished, a strategic stroke aimed at opening up the student quarter, considered hostile to the Imperial régime.

Yet once again, in 1900, the stage was held by an opera about life and love in Bohemia, and Rodolphe and Mimi were exchanged for Julien and Louise, the ill-fated seamstress of Gustave Charpentier's work of that name. By that time, however, Bohemia was frowned upon, and in the 'nineties a proposal to place a bust of Murger in the Luxembourg Gardens caused an outcry in the Press.

Today there is something of the same gaiety and *ennui* about the Quarter, but it smacks of artificiality. The new Bohemian has a nostalgia for something he never knew, and he aspires to relive the past, but his environment and economics have changed: his taste is for *le hot jazz* and espresso coffee; he sleeps o' nights, most often alone; and, unlike his predecessors, he is afraid of ridicule. Even the Existentialists have lost heart.

In a preface to one of his works Baudelaire compared Murger to Musset, both Bohemian classics, though the first spoke of Bohemia with a bitter bantering, and the second, when he was not inspired, had what Arthur Symons called 'crises of fatuity'. Baudelaire went on: 'All this evil society, with its vile habits, its adventurous morals, was painted by the vivid pencil-stroke of Murger, only he jested in his relations of miserable things.'

Let Arthur Symons, the Herrick of the London music-hall in the 'nineties, have the last word:

Yes, Murger is a veracious historian; believe him, if you do not know or have forgotten, that such are the annals of Bohemia. There, people laugh just so lightly and sincerely, weep and laugh just as freely, are really hungry, really have their ambitions, and at times die of all these maladies. It is the gayest and most melancholy country in the world. To have lived there too long is to find all the rest of the world in exile.

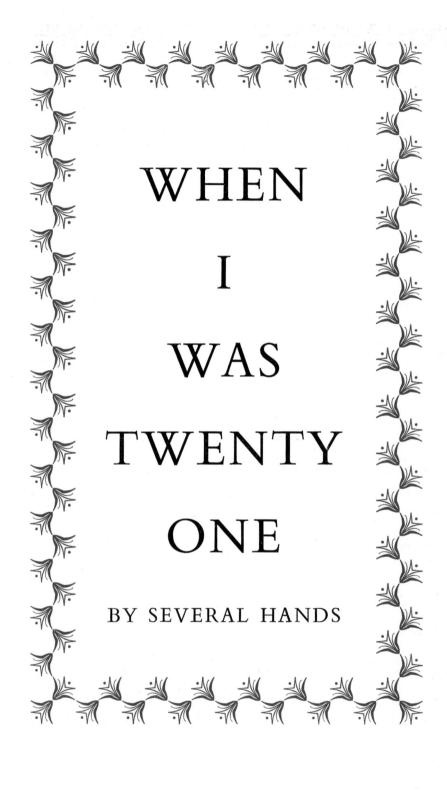

WHEN
I
WAS
TWENTY
ONE

BY SEVERAL HANDS

WHEN I WAS TWENTY-ONE

1898

SIR PHILIP GIBBS

I HAD BEEN in my first job for three years when I was twenty-one, sixty-three years ago. It was with Cassell and Company, the publishers in Ludgate Hill. I advanced upon them each morning in a frock-coat and tall hat, so asserting my social status in the caste system of that time. There must have been something comical about my appearance because I noticed to my embarrassment (being intensely shy) that the workmen in the Belle Sauvage yard, heaving great rolls of paper, winked at one another on my approach.

This may have been due to my look of extreme youth, of which I was very self-conscious. My chief in Cassell and Company, whose room I shared, asked 'Who is that pretty girl?' when such a one popped her head round the door and quickly retreated at the sight of him. I answered blushingly: 'A friend of mine, sir.' I had not the courage to say: 'That is my wife.'

Incredible as it seems to me now, I became a married man in that year, 1898, on a salary of £2 15s. a week.

It was the year before the Boer War. That is a very important period in history, not because of the war itself, which made us hated by most other countries, but because those years of fighting in South Africa divided in a blurred way one world from another—the Old World from the New.

When I was twenty-one we were still unquestionably in the Old World; and it was utterly different from our way of life now.

The traffic which roared down Fleet Street and the Strand was horse-drawn. At night one heard the clip-clop of the hansom cab, the slither of horses' hooves on wet roads, the lash of the whip. In the country, away

from railways, the tempo of life was no faster than the pace of a horse, as it had been for thousands of years. No flying thing disturbed the peace of the sky.

Electric light had not arrived except in some theatres and public halls. As boys, my brothers and I knew an old gentleman named Wimshurst who created waves of electricity by what is still famous as the Wimshurst machine, but the new power was still unavailable for domestic use in 1898. My own home was lit by oil-lamps and candlelight. When my father became tired of his guests he would amuse and exasperate his family by pinching out a candle in the drawing-room, and then another, and another, until dusk threatened darkness and the company took the hint.

There was, of course, no turning on of knobs to produce music or drama or interviews with famous people. Television was beyond imagination. The ordinary middle-class family like mine had to rely on itself for its entertainment. When my mother and father gave an At Home the family and guests provided the programme—but always with pretended reluctance:

'Will you play something, my dear?'

'I'm afraid I left my music behind. I'm so sorry.'

She knew quite well that her husband had brought her music and left it in the hall, as he would remind her when the time came.

I have said that we were an ordinary middle-class family, but, on second thoughts, perhaps we were rather extraordinary. It was because of what the Americans would call our 'cultural' background. Under the influence of my father and mother we read all the great masters of English literature (as well as the *Bow Bells Novelette*, the *Police Gazette*, and *Ally Sloper*, pinched from the servants in the kitchen). As a young boy I was taken by my mother to the old St James's Hall to listen to the 'Monday Pops' in which one heard the greatest musicians of the time, like the violinist Joachim.

My father happened to be a friend of D'Oyly Carte, who owned the Savoy Theatre in which the plays of Gilbert and Sullivan were produced, and he was kind enough to give us the stage-box for each production. We were so close to the stage that we could overhear the private whispers of the players, and they used to smile at us because of our terrific enthusiasm.

When I went into Cassell's I was already dedicated to writing of one

kind or another, and I began to earn a few extra guineas by writing fairy stories for *Little Folks*. But I was encouraged to write my first book by that distinguished man whose room I shared, H. O. Arnold-Forster, Secretary of State for War, and afterwards Secretary for the Navy.

I had been reading a German novel in the art department of the firm when a voice spoke over my shoulder: 'Can you read German?' I turned and saw a tall, good-looking man with the bluest eyes I have ever seen in a human face—china blue.

'I am trying to,' I answered modestly.

'Oh, that's interesting. Come up and see me one day—tomorrow, if you like, at this time.'

'Who's that?' I asked of a colleague when he had gone.

'Good heavens!' he exclaimed. 'That is our chief, a terrifying fellow.'

I did not find him terrifying. I found him very kind and friendly. He asked me to join his own department, which dealt with educational books, and to sit in his room. So I found myself in a spacious apartment at the very top of Cassell's and in the company of a very remarkable man who came in every day for an hour or two. He was always very haughty to distinguished visitors, such as admirals or generals, but if a smudge-nosed office-boy could not find the right room to which to deliver a proof Arnold-Forster would get up from his desk and very graciously help the boy to find it. It was in the same spirit of *noblesse oblige* that he wrote a preface for my first book.

I was still living at home with my father and mother and part of the family. I had to hand over some of my earnings to keep the family pot boiling and it did not leave much margin for my own expenses—midday meals, clothes, cigarettes, fares to Ludgate Hill. Those were the early days of the A.B.C. and Lyons's Tea Shops. For threepence one could quench the pangs of hunger with a bun and a glass of milk. For tenpence one could banquet like a lord on a meat pudding, a fruit tart, and a cup of coffee. For one-and-tuppence, with a penny for the waiter, one could lunch in a real restaurant on roast beef, two vegetables, a sweet, and a cup of coffee.

We were still living in the era of old Fagin and his pickpocket apprentices, Charlie Bates and the Artful Dodger. I became their victim during a Lord Mayor's show. First they relieved me of a handsome tie-pin, next they took a gold watch and chain given to me by my father, and they had unfastened half my cuff-links when my suspicion was aroused and I saw two young scamps scuttling away through the crowd.

[205]

I became very familiar in those days with the London slums. The most terrifying aspect of them was the drunken fights, caused by cheap alcohol, especially between mad-drunk women and the police. It often needed four policemen to overpower one of these viragos and strap her to a wheeled stretcher before trundling her away to the police station.

One saw the most tragic aspect of the slums at night, when numbers of unfortunate people had to sleep on the cold stones. One of the favourite sleeping-places was in the arches under the Adelphi. There the police would not disturb them. They were not allowed to sleep for long on the Embankment seats or in the doorways of shops.

The Salvation Army was the only friend of the down-and-out, and did a work of great charity by providing cheap beds at night and cheap meals by day. The great dormitories were not attractive, and I shuddered when I saw scores of men sleeping in coffin-like beds, snuffling and cough-ing in their sleep, but for them it was a boon to be in such shelter, for which they had to pay only a few pence.

In the slum districts where there was a lot of fighting and drunkenness the public houses were shunned by all respectable women except the Salvation Army lasses in their poke bonnets, tinkling their tambourines and calling upon rough and violent men to repent and believe in the Blood of the Lord. Never were the Salvation Army lasses touched. Fear-lessly also, through the toughest streets of slumdom, where no policeman would walk alone, went hospital nurses in their uniforms.

I came to know the founder of the Salvation Army, old General Booth. He was like a Jewish prophet in modern dress, and was, I think, very near to being a saint. He would make a fool of himself for the love of God, and I have seen him dancing around the stage with old mammies, clap-ping his hands at them. But he could be very fierce in his denunciation of evil, and did not easily forgive any insults to himself or his 'Army'.

When I became a journalist on the *Daily Mail*, Alfred Harmsworth, afterwards Lord Northcliffe, asked me to go down and see the old man, who was annoyed with him for some words that had been written about the 'Army'. The General was still annoyed, but after some conversation he took me by the wrist, forced me down to my knees, and prayed very earnestly for the soul of Alfred Harmsworth. This may have done some good to the proprietor of the *Daily Mail*, but not long afterwards I got the sack.

Hunger and tragic misery lurked in the back streets of London,

inspiring such poems as 'The Song of the Shirt'; but I am bound to recall the astonishing fact that there was a great deal of laughter and good fun among the so-called 'lower classes'. Nothing could have been more rowdy and riotously gay than the procession to Epsom Downs on Derby Day, along the Clapham High Road. It lasted for hours, and was made up of smart coaches filled with sporting ladies and gentlemen, and open vans crowded with coster girls in their huge flowered hats, with their men in 'pearlies', laughing, singing, and shouting—every kind of cart, with four wheels or two, driven by humorists who exchanged endless repartee with the crowd, and every kind of horse, pony, or donkey capable of getting as far as Epsom (some of them wearing ladies' drawers). There was never a pause in the symphony of trumpets, whistles, mouth organs, and accordions, and the human voice raised in ribald song and laughter.

London at that time contained several foreign quarters, and with an amateur photographer from Cassell's I used to explore them during the luncheon hour for the purpose of writing magazine articles. We liked to go to the Italian quarters of London, beyond Holborn. Here we met the old gentleman whose hair curled into crotchets and quavers while he pricked out the tunes and trills on to rolls of cartridge paper which went into piano organs and by the turn of the handle made the music of the street. We went into the haunts of the barrel-organ boys with their scarlet-coated monkeys, both of them exploited by the slave-owners who brought them over.

I wrote an article, published in a London magazine, describing the life of an Italian community who made ice-cream, to be wheeled round in barrows with the cry of 'Okey-pokey, penny a lump'. We became very friendly with these folk, living in a courtyard off Holborn. But when we paid them a second visit, after the publication of the article, their friendliness had disappeared. The Italian women screamed at us. The courtyard filled suddenly with young men who drew their knives and flashed them under our noses. It looked as if we were both going to have our throats cut until a bobby pushed his way into the crowd with the traditional 'Nah then, what's all this 'ere?'

Most of the men disappeared. In those days, unlike today, there was great respect for the police. This bobby learnt from one of the women the cause of the hostility. In my article I had suggested that their cellars were not the most sanitary places for the manufacture of ice-cream. They had taken deep offence. It taught me a lesson as a future journalist.

There was another foreign quarter in London, beyond Aldgate. It was entirely Jewish, and great numbers of the people there—the poorest among them—had fled from Germany and Central Europe and had not yet learnt a word of English. They spoke only Yiddish, as some years later I found out with a friend when we tried to get a night's lodging in their district. They were darkly suspicious of us and thought we were police 'narks'. There was also, of course, a big population of well-to-do Jews in London, and the police told me that they were the most respectable of people, never getting drunk and never neglecting their children.

One of the most picturesque places in London was Hessel Street Market. At night it was lit by flares and the stalls were hung with tapestries, on top of which, cross-legged, sat old oriental Jews with long greasy ringlets. It was like a scene from an Eastern bazaar.

There were many political refugees in London at that time. I came in touch with some of those who had fled from Russia to escape the horrors of Siberia under Tsardom. One group of them was making cigarettes at a factory in the East End. Among them were professors, scientists, lawyers, teachers, and poets.

It seems almost unbelievable now that I talked with an old Russian who was the first man to manufacture cigarettes in England. He had set up his factory in London shortly after the Crimean War, when our young officers had acquired the habit. I met him when he was an old man over ninety. (It may be remembered that Charles Dickens never mentioned cigarette-smoking in any of his novels.)

The pageant of life in London streets has greatly changed. I remember before the Boer War the cheap-jacks, the costers, the Tommies in their scarlet jackets, the crossing sweepers, and the gipsies with the old London cries: 'Buy my pretty lavender, two sprigs a pen-ny.'

Instead of the modern sports car, the smart young fellow of the 'eighties and 'nineties would drive a high dog-cart with a little 'tiger' sitting back-to-back with folded arms.

To get about London one had to use the old horse buses, unless one was rich enough to hire a hansom. They were strewn with straw for the feet on wet days, and soon became damp and dirty. There was no shelter on top from wind or rain. Up there it was considered a privilege to sit next to the driver, who was muffled up in a greatcoat with a heavy scarf round his neck, just like Tony Weller. For family parties coming from the seaside with their luggage there was the old 'growler', and I remember

being shocked as a young boy by a miserable-looking man running after us, for four miles at least, from the station to our house and then asking for sixpence for helping with the luggage.

'The Underground' had been established, but the trains were driven by steam engines, and it needed some pluck and good lungs to survive the terrors of Blackfriars Station with its choking fumes.

Straw was laid down in the streets when some well-to-do person lay a-dying because he might be distressed by the noise of traffic. But it was the lower middle class living in back streets who provided the greatest pageantry when someone died and was buried. I went to the funeral of a traveller in school books for my educational department at Cassell's. A dozen of us sat silently in the parlour with the weeping widow, who was enjoying the occasion in spite of her grief. Presently there arrived a black hearse drawn by four black horses who looked as if they had been dipped in ink. They had high black plumes on their heads. They were noble creatures and high-steppers, accompanied by the funeral master and six mutes all dressed in the deepest black, with black sashes round their tall hats, and black gloves.

'It's just as the poor dear would have liked it,' said the weeping widow, before all of us were provided with black gloves and set forth in carriages behind the hearse, bringing the traffic to a halt until we had passed.

Wandering about London I used to come across some queer characters. One of them was outside a house at the back of Westminster Abbey. I was passing at an early hour in the morning when I was brought to a stop by a big sack which seemed to be moving in a very odd way. 'That's strange,' I thought. 'Perhaps I'm unwell.' At that moment a young man came briskly down the steps. He wore a neat suit, with a bowler hat, and I noticed that his eyes were a yellowy green.

'What's inside that sack?' I asked.

He answered with a smile: 'Would you like to see?'

He put his hands inside the sack and jerked out a live rat.

'Eight hundred of them inside that sack,' he told me.

It appeared from a card he gave me later that he was *Rat-catcher to the City of London.*

In the course of a friendly conversation he told me that the hotels and warehouses along the line of the river were infested by rats and it was his job to keep them down. His technique was simple. He would net the main rooms, like a poacher catching rabbits. Then he would stand perfectly still

O

in the darkness until he heard the patter of feet all round him. Then he would beat the floor with a white wand and make a loud jodelling noise in his throat. The rats would be panic-stricken, and rush in all directions to be caught in the nets. He would sell his night's catch for fourpence a rat to sporting gentlemen in Mitcham.

An old hotel in Fleet Street called Anderson's—destroyed during the Blitz—was one of those which required the attention of my rat-catcher friend. One afternoon I called to the waiter excitedly: 'There's a horrible rat prowling about!'

'Oh, that's old Tom,' said the waiter, not at all perturbed. 'He's quite a friend of mine.'

The rat menace reached a sensational climax when there was a big fire on the south side of the river. Thousands of rats marched in a dense mass across the Strand, advanced up Southampton Street, invaded the shop of Clarkson's, the famous costumier, devoured all his stock, and then occupied Covent Garden market, where in time they were destroyed.

The newspaper offices in and off Fleet Street, about which I wrote a novel called *The Street of Adventure*, were shabby old buildings in the days before their proprietors became noble lords and their editors were knighted. When I first became a journalist the owners and editors thought nothing of having their supper brought round from the nearest pub and eating it in their shirt-sleeves at the editorial desk. But they turned out better newspapers than now, and more of them. Among the dailies, we have lost the *Morning Post* and the *Standard*. Among the evening papers, we no longer have the *Westminster Gazette* or the *Globe* or the *Pall Mall Gazette* or the *Echo*.

London, when I was twenty-one, was a smaller and shabbier but, in my opinion, a pleasanter city than it is now. For me, those monstrous blocks of cement and glass have utterly destroyed its character. But even in my young days London was always growing; and little shops, such as those in Kensington High Street, were becoming big shops like Harrods and Barkers. This process had been going on for half a century. Nevertheless, my mother remembered picking wild flowers in the Edgware Road. I myself remember green fields in Notting Hill Gate. Before 1820 Eaton Square had been made up of market gardens belonging to the Duke of Westminster, and in time to come I owned the last little farmhouse in London—a little old timbered house, which is still there, behind Sloane Square.

WHEN I WAS TWENTY-ONE

1907

SIR HAROLD NICOLSON

IN THE SUMMER of 1907, a few months only before I was twenty-one, my father asked me to be polite to an old friend of his, a professor at the Sorbonne, who was visiting Oxford and wished to obtain some insight into undergraduate life. I gave Professor Duvidier luncheon in my rooms in Broad Street and thereafter walked him round some of the colleges. We ended up on the lawn of the Botanical Gardens gazing down on the Cherwell.

It was a beautiful summer evening; the azaleas and the rhododendrons were still in flower and there was a smell of musk roses in the air. There were punts passing down the river filled with undergraduates and their guests. The men, dressed in white flannel trousers and wearing straw hats and club blazers, handled the wet punt-poles judiciously; the women and the girls, in bright frocks, reclined on plush mattresses amid gaily coloured cushions and held parasols above their heads to preserve their complexions. It was all very Tissot in effect.

'Tell me,' the Professor enquired, 'those women, *ce sont des petites femmes?*'

I blushed scarlet at such a suggestion. 'Of course not,' I replied, indignantly, 'they are sisters or cousins up from London or else the wives and daughters of dons who have been invited on a picnic.'

'*Voyons donc!*' the Professor remonstrated, 'you can't expect me to believe that! Your father told me that you would show me everything in all honesty. You are not being sincere.'

'But I assure you, Professor,' I insisted, 'there are no *filles de joie* in Oxford that I know of; and if there were, no undergraduate would display them in a punt on the Cherwell.'

'*C'est incroyable,*' he muttered. '*Incroyable!*'

'But I assure you that it is so. Take my own contemporaries. There are six or seven of them with whom I am on terms of the frankest intimacy. Yet I assure you, Professor, that all of us, including myself, are complete virgins in so far as women are concerned. I know this to be true.'

'*Ah, ça,*' he growled ferociously, '*ça me révolte.*'

Often, in later years, have I recalled this slight sex-talk beside the Cherwell. Were we, in fact, cases of arrested development? Did we all nourish so sentimental a respect for the innocence of the opposite sex that we regarded any physical approach to them with superstitious horror? And how came it that, whereas at our public schools we had taken un-natural vice as an everyday occurrence, we persisted, even at the age of twenty, in regarding natural vice as irreverent and, in fact, obscene? I had been told by two Greek friends, and by a French friend, that they had made a habit of frequenting brothels from the age of sixteen. These confessions filled me with revulsion. And I could see that they, as well as Professor Duvidier, regarded me as an hypocrite, a liar, or even worse.

I have often reflected that the virginity of English undergraduates may account for many unsatisfactory marriages and broken homes. We had, I suppose, inherited the Victorian legend that all women were pure as driven snow and that it was solely owing to the sweet dutifulness of their nature that (meek unconscious doves) they surrendered their limbs to the embraces of the male. It would have shocked us deeply had we been told that a woman also might derive pleasure from lust. In such matters the young Englishmen of my generation were as cold, as clumsy, and I suppose as selfish, as Swedes.

It is a mystery to me why our ignorance in sex matters did not lead to more unhappiness and greater perversions than it did. I do not recall that at the age of twenty-one I was in any way as troubled by sexual desire as I was at the age of twenty-four. I may have been a late-flowering plant, but if that be so, then all my contemporaries were also Michaelmas daisies rather than primroses. There was, it is true, an Hungarian Count at Magdalen who would boast loudly about his adventures with women. We regarded him as very Central European. We even blushed. I doubt whether men of twenty-one today possess a similar sense of shame. I can assure them that it is inhibiting; and may lead to very unfortunate results.

It wasn't as if my own background and training had been so very

Anglican. My father was in the diplomatic service. I had been born in Persia and was brought up in Turkey, Hungary, Morocco, Spain, and Russia. My first nurse had been a male attendant from the Bakhtiari Mountains of the name of Firuz. My second nurse was a German woman of the name of Anna. Then Miss Plimsoll arrived and my conditioning became very British indeed. But the esoteric incense of my first nursery hung about my childhood. In some way it rendered it difficult for me, when at The Grange, Folkestone, and subsequently at Wellington College, to feel or even to behave exactly the same as all the other boys. Had I been very deft at games I might have mastered this outsider feeling; but I was not deft at games. By the time I was twenty-one I yearned desperately, and as I now think unnecessarily, to conform to the pattern set me by the Etonians, the Marlburians, and Wykehamists whose attitude of unflaunting self-assurance I so much admired at Balliol.

Until I entered the Foreign Office at the age of twenty-two, my only contact with the habits and standards of the Anglo-Saxon landed gentry was provided during the Easter holidays, which I would spend with my uncle and aunt in Northern Ireland. It was there that I was taught by the gamekeeper to kill rabbits, and by the house-carpenter to despise the Pope of Rome. The London mail, I remember, would in those days arrive at eleven in the morning, when the family and the guests would gather in the library to receive their letters, to glance at the newspapers, and to consume a glass of Marsala and a slice of seed cake. In those days I was highly strung, and it took many years of diverse experience before I mastered my nerves. Until over the age of thirty I was frightened alone at night; I was atrociously self-conscious and shy; and until the age of fifty-three I suffered much from hypochondria, by which I do not mean the melancholy that so afflicted my kinsman James Boswell, but actual health-fuss and dread of death. I was always feeling my pulse and detecting within my body the stirrings of some mortal disease.

On one occasion, I remember, having just returned from Russia, I became convinced that in the Nord Express from St Petersburg I had contracted diabetes. Walking sadly to the National Gallery, where I hoped by the contemplation of beauty to divert my mind from my approaching death, I found it necessary once again to descend to the lavatory under Trafalgar Square. My illness, evidently, was gaining on me by leaps and bounds. I decided that if after gazing at the Titians I again felt bound to take refuge below street level, I should immediately place myself in the

[213]

hands of a doctor. Thus, when on leaving the Gallery I had again to descend, I hailed a hansom cab and told the driver to go to Harley Street, which I had heard was the region where doctors abounded. On leaving my cab, I rang the bell at the first door which bore a brass plate announcing that Dr So-and-so lived within. I was admitted to the presence. 'Well, young man,' said the doctor cheerfully, 'what can I do for you?' 'I am afraid,' I replied modestly, 'that I have got diabetes.' He laughed at that. 'But what on earth,' he said, 'induced you to consult me? I am a dermatologist.' I explained that my parents lived abroad, that I had no family doctor, and that I had rung at the first brass-plated door in Harley Street more or less on the chance. He was a benevolent man and consented to take the necessary tests. 'I can assure you,' he said, 'that you have not got a sign of diabetes. But you have been overworking. I advise you to consult my friend Dr Brown, who is a general practitioner.' So off I went to Sloane Street, and I have not, so far, contracted diabetes again.

Owing to such diffidence, doubts, and anxieties, I cannot say that at the age of twenty-one I was as happy as I have been ever since the age of twenty-four. I loved my last two years at Oxford, but owing to arrested development I was lamentably lazy and did not gain the academic distinctions to which I might have aspired. I have never been lazy since, knowing from experience that indolence is the root-cause of melancholy. 'Happiness is activity,' wrote the Master of Them that Know, and I agree that failure, even to tie one's shoe-laces tightly, is a source of self-reproach and gloom. The melancholy that assailed me when I was twenty-one was not due entirely to my anxieties and sense of insufficiency, but also to a phase of laziness. The moment I started to work really hard my depression passed, and during the years after I left Oxford, the years from the age of twenty to the age of twenty-three, I worked very hard indeed.

I was preparing for the entrance examination into the Diplomatic Service and was resolved to compensate by my success in that examination for my contemptible performance in the Oxford schools. Only barely had I obtained a degree. Thus during the years 1906–9 I would go abroad to learn foreign languages and live for three months or so in some French or German or Italian home. It was in the spring of 1908, when I was twenty-one years and six months old, that I experienced the full onslaught of that terrible malady which brought the young Werther to his death and which, owing to that episode I suppose, is known as 'Weltschmerz'.

[214]

I had been working hard at Siena, living with a charming family of the name of Grottanelli, reading history all afternoon and evening, and taking lessons in the morning from a priest. He had rooms opposite the Cathedral and I would walk round there in the morning carrying my copybook and the exercise in translation that I had done the night before. He was a nice priest and his rooms were spotless, shining and heavily scented with the narcissus which his parishioners would bring him from the fields, and which were massed on the tiled floor of his study in large earthenware jars. We would read Dante together, and Leopardi, and Carducci, since he was a broad-minded priest and had no prejudices against anti-clerical poets. When dark descended and my eyes became weary from too much reading, I would pass through one of the great pink gates of Siena and walk rapidly (since I must surely 'take exercise') on the silent hills around. After three months of this regular and austere timetable I was invited by an Oxford friend of mine, Enrico Visconti Venosta, to stay at a sumptuous villa at Fiesole belonging to one of his grand friends. I felt shabby, ungainly, and inarticulate in these rich and vivacious surroundings. It was a lovely spring, and we dined on the terrace of the villa, looking down on Florence with its lights and dim shapes. The fireflies danced around us and the glow-worms glowed. All the other guests were witty and informative: I felt like a clod of earth:

> Le soir était plus beau qu'on imagine,
> J'avais pitié de moi.

The past seemed ashes to me; all that the future had to offer were further truckloads of ashes succeeding one another in desolate similitude. Moreover, I was afraid that while walking outside the night walls of Siena I had contracted cholera. Never have I suffered from Weltschmerz as I did that evening. And now I am seventy-four years of age; and Riri Visconti, at the age of sixty, joined the resistance forces in Italy and was blown to pieces by a mine. It is a source of pride to me to recall how many of those of my Oxford friends who came from foreign countries lost their lives in resisting Fascist tyranny. It is of men like Riri Visconti and Albrecht Bernstorff that my *alma mater* should feel most proud.

For the remainder of that year I studied either with Jeanne de Hénaut in Paris or with the Lahmeyer family in Hanover. It was in Jeanne de

Hénaut's flat in the Rue de la Pompe that I met Coleridge Kennard, who was then at the summit of his hopes of grandeur. He was beautiful, he was rich, and he was so talented that the *Westminster Gazette* had printed three or four of his poems in prose. His mother, Mrs Carew, had been an intimate friend of Oscar Wilde, and Roy took me one wet afternoon to see the Hôtel d'Alsace where Wilde had died. He also introduced me to Robbie Ross, who in his turn introduced me to Max Beerbohm and Reggie Turner, as well as to 'our coming literary Messiah', Hugh Walpole. Roy Kennard was a year older than I was and was to take his examination that August. When this ordeal was over he went off on a holiday to Venice accompanied by one of Wilde's two sons. He asked me to come to the Gare de Lyons and to talk with him as the express passed through. We sat there at the little bistro on the platform, sipping anisette. It was a wonderful night and a round harvest moon glared into the dark shadows of the station from under the glass roof. I said goodbye to them and the great train slid out under the moon, while Roy, with his golden hair and his elegance, leant out of the gangway, waving: he passed on and away to ease and glory. I was so jealous of his splendour, and of his having finished with the cramming of which a whole other year opened before me, that I decided to ease my sunken spirits by walking back the whole way to the Place Victor Hugo. The moon glittered in the locks, the canals, the basins, and the river itself. All along the *quais* I walked, a lonely little figure, and past the Louvre. '*J'avais pitié de moi*' all over again. I have seldom found the full moon conducive to elation. Thirty-seven years later Roy Kennard, who scarcely fulfilled his early promise, was caught by the Nazis in the south of France and imprisoned in an internment camp. When I last saw him, shortly before his death, he was a sick man; the sheen had left his golden hair.

I have written elsewhere about Jeanne de Hénaut and the cramming establishment in the Rue de la Pompe. I owe her much. The atmosphere of the pension kept by the Lahmeyers in Hanover was more sedative and domestic. Old Frau Lehmeyer, or 'Frau Bürgomeister' as we used to call her, was a gentle and faded widow, and the establishment was run by her married daughter Frau Ermine Abentern, also a widow, and by her younger daughter, the spinster Lilli. Ermine had lost her husband some years previously and would assure us with pride that many officers had attended her husband's funeral. She would also indulge in snatches of song:

Da geh' ich ins Maxim
Da bin ich sehr intime . . .

The Frau Bürgomeister did not approve of this singing. 'Ermine,' she would mutter, complainingly, *'sei doch nicht so frivole.'* Lilli was a dear little woman who had a soul. During the last month of my stay in Hanover she became convinced that I had fallen in love with some girl from the Blumensäle. I hadn't fallen in love, and in fact my visits to the Blumensäle had been few and far between. But so convinced was Lilli of this disastrous love affair that she refrained from seeing me off at the station when I left for a holiday in Russia; she feared that I might be embarrassed in bidding farewell to the Blumensäle if she were also there. She need not have had such fear.

My sex instincts, as I have said, were in those days undeveloped. I had no religious convictions. I had been confirmed at Wellington and had during twelve hours experienced some spasms of religious ecstasy. But they had passed away in the rough-and-tumble of school life, and all that I took to Oxford was the congenital puritanism that I have retained ever since. I believe that my political opinions would also have remained conventional had it not been that during my rare vacations I stayed with my parents in the Embassy at St Petersburg. It was this ghastly experience which first converted me to Socialism. I only once saw the Tsar and his wife, when they came up by boat to the capital to preside at the ceremony of Blessing of the Waters. The ice on the Neva, which for the previous four months had concealed beneath its scab the gaiety of its rushing splendour, had begun to break up; it was obligatory on the Tsar to bless at a liturgical ceremony the release of those buoyant waters. He walked from the winter palace across the quay to a small baroque pavilion erected out into the river. He then performed some ceremony of aspersion which those watching from the palace windows were unable to see, owing to the mists of incense, the awning which enclosed the pavilion, and the golden copes of bowing archimandrites and metropolitans. The Tsar seemed to me a gay and amiable man; the Tsaritsa, with her jaundiced eyes, with her head bent low so as to conceal the fact that she was taller than her husband, appeared as melancholy as Niobe. None of us could, in that spring afternoon of 1908, foresee the massacre that took place ten years later in the house of the engineer Ipatiev.

Our hopes in those days were fixed on the Prime Minister, Stolypin, who was a man of immense physical courage and enlightened views. We believed that he would succeed in creating a great class of peasant proprietors who would provide Russia with the foundation of bourgeois stability which she so sadly lacked. Here again we did not foresee that the influence of Peter Arkadievich Stolypin would be undermined by court intrigues and vested interests, or that he would, with his great mission incomplete, be shot dead by a Jew in the theatre at Kiev.

I was, at the age of twenty-one, deeply moved by the contrast that in those days existed in Russia between rich and poor. My father, in the hope of teaching me some Russian, engaged a student to go for walks with me in the cobbled streets of that superb city. He was a man with nail-brush hair, huge hands, and a gentle voice. One afternoon we passed a beggar squatting on the pavement with a tattered cap beside him. I threw some money into the cap, but my teacher reproved me angrily 'for despising the poor'. I was so impressed by his anger that I returned to my beggar, rescued my half-rouble, took off my hat, and going on one knee beside him replaced the coin gently in his cap. The beggar and my student-tutor were equally surprised by this Tolstoian genuflexion. My teacher was encouraged by this episode to confess to me that he was a social revolutionary and longed for the day when Tsardom would fall. I pleaded rather mildly for my hero Stolypin, but my defence of that great man was met with scorn. 'How can you abide,' my teacher said to me, 'to live in such luxury, when there is tyranny around you and appalling cold and hunger among the poor?'

I admit that the luxury in those days was overpowering. In the wide courtyard of the Embassy there was a mountain of sawn birch logs, which were used to heat the furnace, which, through brass orifices, or *bouches de feu*, inserted into the silk hangings, would pump hot air into the saloons. I can remember, on the eve of some reception, going into the long supper-room of the Embassy and finding there six footmen in their liveries having their hair powdered by a hairdresser. The upper part of their bodies was swathed in linen sheets; their brown plush knickers, their yellow silk stockings, and their lacquer shoes and gold buckles protruded below. Each of the footmen held in his hand an enormous cone of cardboard with which he covered his features while the powder was being puffed onto his pomaded head. It was a disgusting spectacle. I returned to my mother's boudoir angry and sick of soul.

What distressed me even more were the occasions when I was invited

to a ball in winter at one of the great houses. The air was so desiccated by the *bouches de feu* that footmen would circulate round the ballroom spraying scented water on the guests. The rooms were banked with azaleas; the dresses of the women came straight from Paris; the uniforms of the men sparkled with jewelled stars. In the courtyards of these palaces the coachmen would wait while the frost gathered on their beards and their breath steamed like a samovar. I minded this very much.

The Menshevik sentiments that such experiences aroused in me have persisted ever since, and today render me a loyal follower of Mr Gaitskell. They were reinforced by the police system which quite overtly existed around us. We knew that the Embassy porter was in the pay of the police and that he would obediently report to headquarters the names of all those who visited the Embassy. This rendered it impossible for my father to have any contact with the leading members of the opposition, then known as 'The Octobrists' and the 'Constitutional Democrats' or 'Cadets'. An Ambassador who even spoke to a member of the opposition was regarded at Tsarskoe as a *persona non grata*. The French Ambassador, who disregarded this prejudice, was denounced by his porter and had to be recalled. My father was more ingenious. He summoned to his side Sir Donald MacKenzie Wallace, who had written the classic work on Russia, who spoke Russian with the utmost fluency, who was a close personal friend of King Edward VII, and on terms of tried intimacy with such liberal leaders as Heyden, Stakhovitch, and Prince Lvov. The Tsarist police could scarcely arrest Sir Donald MacKenzie Wallace; this eminent expert provided my father with much inside information on Russian conditions which he could not by any other means safely have obtained.

In some strange way these prohibitions, and the resultant stratagems and subterfuges, shocked me more than anything else. Naturally, I agreed with my Russian teacher that only the Duma, under the guidance of liberal statesmen, could prevent a revolution. The only difference between us was that I wanted to see a constitutional democracy and he wanted a red revolution, such as he obtained. I wonder whether he still lives. He was a fine young man and I owe him, apart from a sprinkling of the Russian language as light as the powder which descended on the pomaded heads of the six footmen, some understanding of how a police state can infuriate the young.

The odd thing was that my experience in Russia not only confirmed my hatred of dictatorship and police states but left me, as a humanist,

with a dislike of Russia and the Slavs themselves. Even when I would in summer sit on the balcony, looking down on the sparkling blue Neva and admiring the slim pencil-spire of St Peter and St Paul, it would be the placid Turgenev that I would read rather than the unreasonable and much too excessive Dostoievsky. How smug, how smug, was I at the age of twenty-one! I see myself as a stout, flabby, snobbish little person with curly nose and hair, affable but foolish—not in the least the sort of person with whom I would wish to dine at the Beefsteak Club today.

The following year, at the age of twenty-two, I passed my examination into the diplomatic service. I went to Venice. I went to Spain and Constantinople. I have been happy since; not too often frightened at night; not so shy as to be unable to manage the wriggling of my arms and legs; not tortured by doubts regarding the nature of the Holy Trinity; and quite certainly a liberal Socialist. Much as I should have liked to have been a senator in the age of Hadrian, I think I prefer my own period, in spite of the atrocities and dangers by which it has been faced. Certainly I experienced fear and anger at the contemplation of Mussolini and Hitler; certainly I hated the falling bombs; but on the whole the perplexities of my generation were less terrifying than the doubts which assailed Pascal, Sénancourt, or Arthur Hugh Clough. They were tortured by such doctrines as redemption and original sin; they were afraid they might be denied salvation and condemned to eternal punishment. I was physically frightened only, and physical fear passes.

Yet if I could reverse the hands of time, I should wish to be thirty-two again, not twenty-one.

WHEN I WAS TWENTY-ONE

1920

BEVERLEY NICHOLS

I
T USED to be said of Torquay that most of its inhabitants had gone
down there to die, only to discover when they arrived that they
proceeded most obstinately to live. This may have been a rumour
put about by a Press agent, but it was borne out by the facts when I
was twenty-one. The pretty, lush, muggy resort, built on seven hills
—('like Rome,' we used to boast to one another)—abounded in the rich,
the eccentric, and the elderly—particularly the elderly. A large number
of the residents, when rising for the National Anthem on public occasions,
found themselves automatically lapsing into 'God Save the Queen'. I
remember smiling when one old lady confessed to me that the best she
could manage was a sort of irreverent compromise: 'God Save the Quing'.

There must therefore be a distinctly Edwardian flavour to these
recollections. Although the year was 1920 the casual visitor might have
been excused for fancying himself in 1910. The holocaust of the First
World War had scarcely ruffled the palm trees on the Rock Walk; the
economies which had been forced on the rest of the country had not
snipped an inch off the long white ribbons which floated behind the
aprons of the 'house-parlourmaids' as they hurried to answer the front
doors. No . . . perhaps that is an exaggeration, for the very word 'house-
parlourmaid' was in itself an admission that things were not quite as they
should be. In the old days people in our 'social position' did not have
'house-parlourmaids'. They had a house-maid, a parlourmaid, and a cook.
To combine the functions of two domestics in the person of one was
obviously a significant concession to the new world that was springing
up around us. It was like going to church in a side-car when one had
been used to going in a Daimler.

We lived in a large early-Victorian house in the Lower Warberry Road, and you will not be surprised to learn that it was called Cleave Court. Its original name was merely 'Cleave', but we were so surrounded by 'Courts' and 'Halls' and 'Lodges' and even 'Towers' that my father decided that we had better become a 'Court' too. After all, we were quite as large as 'Warberry Court', which was slightly higher up the hill, and our background was as respectable as that of the Egerton-Edwards, who inhabited it. And we were even larger than Fern Hall, which ran parallel with the bottom of our garden.

There were two things about the owner of Fern Hall which I must ask you to believe, though I do not expect you to do so. Firstly, she was called Miss Tessa Faithful. (This appeared on her visiting cards as Mi*f*s Te*f*sa-Faithful.) Secondly, she kept sixteen laughing jackasses. The maniac chuckle of these creatures, floating up the hill, formed a macabre accompaniment to many hours of my early life, which was not a happy one, to put it mildly. Ours was a house of sadness, and I can think of no sound more fitting as a musical background than the harsh, mirthless comment of the sixteen jackasses. However, it is not on such matters, in this essay, that I wish to dwell.

So 'Cleave Court' it became, and my father, having named it, decided that now was the time to use the family crest. All the 'nicer' residents of Torquay had crests on their writing-paper—spears and clenched fists and arrows and mythological beasts, stamped at great expense on the back of envelopes. Where my father discovered ours I shall never know, but it happened to be quite genuine, and very impressive it looked when it duly appeared. It was a boar's head, surmounting the motto *Spero Meliora*, and whenever I read those words I thought how poignantly apposite they were, particularly for my mother. She had no alternative but to hope for better things; it was scarcely conceivable, during most of her life, that things could have been worse.

As I said before, although the year was 1920, Torquay—or at any rate that section of it in which we moved and had our being, revolving round the Lower Warberry Road—was firmly entrenched in 1910. Thus, it was still the period of 'At Home' days. On the visiting cards of every lady—every *real* lady, that is to say—was printed a mysterious announcement such as 'First and Third Tuesdays', or 'Second Fridays'. When, as a little boy, I first read this cryptic message on one of my own mother's cards

(we were 'First Wednesdays') I was filled with apprehension. It suggested that some strange secret rites were in preparation . . . as indeed, in a sense, they were.

A considerable amount of formal ceremonial practice was associated with the cards themselves. Thus, it was essential that they should be *engraved*; to have had cards *printed* would have stamped their owners as beyond the pale. Again, the cards of the ladies must always be precisely one-third larger than the cards of the gentlemen. Two sizes of black edging were customary in cases of mourning—a thick heavy one for use during the six months immediately following the funeral, and a very thin, almost invisible one for the six months after that.

If a lady was accompanied by her husband they both left one card; if she came alone she left one card for herself and two cards for him. Why this should be I was never able to ascertain. Nor can I remember the precise circumstances which demanded that the top left-hand corner of the card should be turned down, though I fancy it implied that the visitor had called personally, and had not left it to be delivered by an underling.

Sometimes the cards were marked, in the bottom right-hand corner, with the letters 'P.P.C.'—*Pour prendre congé* . . . indicating that the caller was about to leave the district for a long holiday. And sometimes there were purely personal symbols, which could be understood only by a select few. It was the habit of one old lady, if she had not heard for some time from the people on whom she was calling, to write the mystic letters 'N.W.I.H.' These stood for 'Nothing wrong, I hope?'

The cards were deposited on a tray which was handed to the caller by a parlourmaid. The tray, of course, was made of silver, and was always kept brilliantly polished. It was usually engraved, in the centre, with the owner's crest. (In our case it was engraved with somebody else's, because the tray had been bought second-hand. There were long discussions as to whether we should buy a new tray, and put *Spero Meliora* on it, but we never did.) When a sufficient number of cards had been collected they were placed in a large bowl on the hall table, where they were furtively scanned by other callers. It was remarkable how the cards of any titled ladies and gentlemen seemed to float to the top.

As I look back on those 'At Homes', over this considerable span of years, it occurs to me that they involved almost as much fuss and anxiety as a Lord Mayor's banquet. First, there was the matter of the cakes. The

standby was invariably a sort of lemon meringue, which had burst upon Torquay some ten years before in the guise of 'German Cake'. And 'German Cake' it remained, and we all gorged ourselves upon it until the outbreak of hostilities in 1914. Whereupon, needless to say, it was banned from our tea-tables. We would have choked if we had eaten 'German Cake'. The unfortunate confectioner who had created this delicacy was the recipient of a large number of anonymous letters, some of which suggested that he was personally responsible for the wholesale rape of mother superiors in Belgian convents which—as all historians now acknowledge—was the main preoccupation of the Kaiser's High Command.

Apart from the 'German Cake'—which in the year 1919 made a welcome reappearance as 'Swiss Cream'—there were usually two sorts of toasted scones, one with currants and one without. It was essential that these should be home-made. To provide one's guests with scones that had been bought was considered a sign of vulgarity. One might buy 'German Cake', or coffee cake, or chocolate biscuits at the confectioner's, but never scones. People would think that one had not got a cook.

There were always two varieties of tea, Indian and China, and when one was asked which one would have it was more genteel to reply 'China', even if one did not like it. There was cream as well as milk, and lemon as well as sugar. Each plate was provided with a little napkin. Perhaps the pleasantest accompaniment of these parties was the gentle hiss of the hot-water kettle which stood in the centre of most of our tables. As a rule, it was an elaborate creation of Victorian silver, and it was heated by a spirit-lamp built into the framework. The lighting of this lamp, the regulation of its violet flame, and its occasional extinction when it got out of control . . . all these made an agreeable background to conversation.

However, the most urgent concern of the hostess at these strange assemblies was elsewhere. It did not matter so much about the cakes or the scones. Nor the state of the carpet, which in our case was so shabby that a log basket had to be permanently clamped over a hole by the fire-place. Nor the behaviour of the spirit-lamp; nor the arrangement of the flowers. (We were, mercifully, still a long way from the Monstrous Regiment of Female Flower Arrangers.)

What *was* vital—what gave an 'At Home' a cachet or stamped it as

a failure—what made my mother say 'I think they enjoyed themselves'. or left her pathetically wondering and worrying—was the behaviour of the parlourmaid. And I would like you to note that on these occasions it was generally agreed, by a sort of tacit Torquay understanding, that one was shown in through the front door, helped off with one's coat, and served with one's 'German Cake'—pardon me, 'Swiss Cream'—by a *parlourmaid*. Period. Not a 'house-parlourmaid'. In these rosy, fire-lit moments of illusion, when the members of our little society gathered together—so elderly, so 'nice', so forlorn, so creaking, so pointless, so lost, and so heartbreakingly aware, in their secret selves, that they were all these things—it could never be admitted that there was ever such a being as a 'house-parlourmaid'. That would have been a final confession of failure. Even if she were a 'temporary', hired for the day at a fee of five shillings, she was invested, by general consent, with the full rank. And both the hostess and the guests behaved as if, somewhere in the background, she was being supported by the rearguard of a housemaid and a cook. And maybe even a bootboy.

Which reminds me that we once had a bootboy, though that was just before the war. I would not mention this emblem of social success were it not for one remark which he made to me in the summer of 1914. There had been some argument about his wages. I went out to the toolshed to commiserate with him. He spat viciously on a pair of brogues. 'Things is different,' he said. 'And things is *going* to be different.'

He spoke more truly than he knew.

In 1920, however, 'things', for the most part, were not different in the Lower Warberry Road; they were unnaturally, even uncannily, pre-war, though the residents would never have admitted it. *They* imagined that they were living in the full flood of revolution. To prove it, they would only have had to point to the uniforms of the aforesaid house-parlourmaids. Gone were the days of universal black; we were living in swifter, more stirring, times. It was now permissible for the slaves to be garbed in dark grey, or navy, or even a deep and gloomy sort of plum. This was, indeed, my mother's choice for our treasure, May, and on the day that she presented May with her new frock—down to the ankles and rather tight at the waist—they were both as thrilled as a mother and daughter engaged in the pleasing task of choosing a honeymoon trousseau.

But plum—or was it sloe?—was as far as my mother felt inclined to

P

venture. Not for her the excesses of one of our neighbours, Madame de Runkel, whose parlourmaid was suddenly, and suspiciously, attired in pale grey. This, my mother proclaimed, looked positively 'French', and in those days to be 'French' was to be immoral. The fact that Madame de Runkel was firmly, and proudly, Dutch, made no difference at all. Her parlourmaid *looked* French. Besides, Madame de Runkel had central heating. That was another black mark. There was something not quite nice about central heating. Or so we assured ourselves, as we scorched our bottoms by the fireside.

I find myself in a Betjeman mood—a mood when names make music. Names like *Sir St Vincent Hammick*. He was one of the stars of our tea-parties, and my mother told me that he had once been an admiral, though his appearance was far from nautical. With his untidy white hair and his velvet-collared jacket he looked like an elderly 'cellist whose repertoire was limited to the death-throes of the Swan. He used to come with his wife, and my mother always had an uneasy moment when the door was opened to admit them, in case the maid got their names wrong, which she usually did. However long my mother rehearsed her in the morning 'Sir St Vincent and Lady Hammick' was a phrase which seldom came trippingly from her lips. There was one occasion when in sheer desperation she opened the door, cried, 'The 'Ammicks,' and fled. It was fortunate that both Sir St Vincent and his lady were slightly deaf.

The Betjeman mood persists; names come flocking back, like the toll of bells over a distant valley. *Violet Tweedale* was another of our social stars. She was a stately lady who lived in a rather grand house called Villa Maggiore higher up the hill. She had a high bosom and snow-white hair, and she modelled herself on Queen Marie of Rumania. She made a great deal of money out of novels of quite exceptional silliness which were always prominently displayed in the local libraries. When she could not think of a plot for a novel she wrote about ghosts and 'auras', and she once alarmed my mother by telling her that May (the 'treasure') had such a bright aura that she could see it in the dark.

Then there were the *Misses Bateman*, who were always arriving, or departing, from *Flint*. The reader will require an interpretation of this mysterious phrase. He will find it in the yellowing files of the *Torquay Directory*, which published a weekly chronicle of our social activities. One of its most popular columns was concerned with 'arrivals' and

[226]

'departures', and those with a hankering for publicity availed themselves freely of its services. Evidently the Misses Bateman came into this category, for hardly a week passed without our being informed that the Misses Bateman had 'arrived' at their residence, which was called 'Flint' . . . only to learn, in the next issue, that they had again 'departed'. This greatly mystified my father, as well it might, for outwardly the Misses Bateman gave no indication that they might be birds of passage; they were elderly, sedate, even sedentary. 'Where do they *go*?' stormed my father. 'What do they *do*?' Nobody ever found out.

Some of these names have a strange, unearthly quality, as though I had made them up. But nobody, surely, could make up names like *Lancelot* and *Undine Wiggin*? They were real people, and very charming ones. I wonder, as Noël Coward might say, what happened to *them*? And to *Ernestine Appleby*—dear Ernestine who used to sing 'I'm Just Seventeen' to my accompaniment on an ancient Broadwood grand piano. And *Pearl Prout*, with whom I used to dance? Even the names of the houses were often startling and unexpected . . . like Castel à Mare, the haunted house which lurked behind a thick screen of macracarpa at the far end of the road. It bore no resemblance to a castle, and I doubt if one could have seen the sea even from the roof. But one could see a great many other things, horrid things, wicked things, as I know from personal experience. But nobody ever saw as much as Violet Tweedale, who saw a man with an aura that was jet black. And that, she assured us, was about as near to the devil as you could get.

Such was life in Torquay, in the year of grace 1920.

However, the wind of change was on its way, sweeping down from the North, where the post-war prosperity so confidently prophesied by the politicians seemed tardy in arrival. As yet, Torquay was scarcely conscious of any change in temperature. We were sheltered by our seven hills; we could still comfort ourselves by the Roman analogy. But there were times when some of the more thoughtful residents remembered, with a twinge of malaise, that even Rome had suffered a decline and fall.

And then there were the winters. Surely they were not as warm as in the past? The mimosa trees in the Rock Walk—so pleasant to visit on a February morning after church—were they not late in blossoming? And only too often there were white horses on the waters of Torbay.

Moreover, something disturbing was happening in the Lower Warberry Road, and in the Middle and Upper Warberries too. Little by little the Halls were being deserted, the Towers were toppling, and the Courts were closing their gates. Not only closing them, but opening them again, after a suitable period for alterations and decorations, in the role of . . . boarding-houses! Fortunately these changes came gradually; but from the outset they were resented. The idea of a boarding-house in the Lower Warberry Road was unsupportable, even though some of the boarders, so we were told, were quite 'nice' people. For a long time after its appearance the older residents, when they passed it, would hasten their steps and avert their eyes, as they had done when passing Castel à Mare. Ghosts were bad enough . . . but boarders!

Meanwhile, though we were still able for the most part to 'keep ourselves to ourselves', we could hardly be unaware of a new and sinister mood in the country at large, particularly in the country's youth. There was, for example, a terrible trio called the Sitwells, who wrote 'free' verse that had neither rhyme nor reason, and who associated with the most Bohemian persons . . . all the more extraordinary because they came from a family which was eminently 'nice'. And there was a young man called Aldous Huxley whose short stories really should not be allowed in any public library. Somebody should speak to Boots' about it. And there was another young man called Noël Coward, a notorious drug fiend who lived in a permanent haze of narcotics. Our one consolation was that such indulgence would necessarily put a speedy end to his career.

Perhaps the most dangerous of all this raffish crew was young Beverley Nichols. It was difficult to believe that he could have had the advantages of a Torquay background or that he could have come from such a 'nice' home. (The laughing jackasses could have made a fitting comment on *that*.) Only the year before, in 1919, when Mr Nichols was President of the Union at Oxford, he had actually advocated a system of Soviets among the undergraduates! Why was he not sent down by the authorities? And with him, his revolutionary companions, including one Leslie Hore-Belisha, a name which spoke for itself in the most menacing accents. No wonder the *Morning Post* (the only really *decent* paper, for even *The Times* was not all it should be) proclaimed in flaring headlines the arrival of BOLSHEVISM AT OXFORD.

As if that were not enough, Mr Nichols, the twenty-one-year-old Lenin in embryo, had now published a novel! Mind you, there was no harm in publishing a novel, even at so early an age, provided it was a

[228]

'nice' novel. But *Prelude*[1] could not possibly be included in this category. It had been condemned in that splendid new paper, the *Sunday Express*— again in flaring headlines—as POISONOUS FROM COVER TO COVER. By whom? By no less a person than Mr James Douglas, one of the great moral forces of the times, almost as potent in his prose and as impeccable in his sentiments as Horatio Bottomley himself—always swift on the trail of evil, ruthless in his exposure of vice—as he was to prove, a few years later, in his fearless, single-handed attack on Miss Radclyffe Hall's *Well of Loneliness*. (Here again he was to use the poison metaphor—such an artist of words!—proclaiming that he would rather that his daughter swallowed a vial of prussic acid than read such a book.)

And to think that all these years, in the person of Beverley Nichols, Torquay had been nursing a viper in its bosom! One really should *cut* the awful young man. And one *would*, if it were not for his charming father. But at least one could 'speak to Boots'' about it. And one did.

Dear Torquay! From time to time my journeys take me there again; but I do not linger, for the place is totally unrecognizable. Not physically. The sea is still blue at Babbacombe Bay; in the neighbourhood of the Imperial Hotel one can still capture a faint if somewhat chilly illusion of the Riviera; the mimosa still blooms fitfully in the Rock Walk; and the seven hills still stand proudly round Torbay. But the noise! And—if Torquay will forgive me for saying so—the people! No doubt they are charming and young and lusty—an admirable advertisement for the Welfare State, as they devour their fish-and-chips from plastic bags on the beach. And maybe the young novelist who wrote *Prelude* might have found some agreeable companions among them, to whom he might have imparted his poisonous doctrines.

But the ageing author of these words feels nothing but a faint regret. No doubt they were absurd, these spectral figures whom I have evoked. No doubt they were futile. But they had a certain elegance. And when they were faced with tragedy they met it with dignity and restraint. They rose above the cackle of the laughing jackasses.

Well . . . it does not matter so much, does it? Most of them are dead and gone. In more senses than one, the Misses Bateman have departed, for ever, from Flint.

---

[1] A little school story which still occasionally brings me nostalgic letters from Old Marlburians

WHEN I WAS TWENTY-ONE

1928

LOUIS MACNEICE

O N MY twenty-first birthday I was depressed. Apart from a pair of gold cuff-links, bought for me in Belfast (that Northern anti-Athens), there was no celebration, and there was another month to go before I could escape from the puritanism and mud of my Ulster surroundings to the honey-coloured finials and gilded understatements of Oxford, where I was still *in statu pupillari*. The Long Vacation of 1928 had seemed a waste of time. I had been made to accompany my father, then a Church of Ireland archdeacon, on a Cook's Tour in and out of the fjords of Norway on a liner where one had to dress for dinner—and in a stiff shirt at that—and where people under forty were a small minority. There was on board one American group of young men and women—the kind my family would have described as 'fast'—who spent their days playing 'Dance, Dance, Dance, Little Lady' on a portable gramophone, but I was much too throttled by my father's dog-collar to try to get to know them. So I pretended I had no wish to know them and sent one of my fellow Old Marlburians a postcard saying '*Qu'allais-je faire dans cette galère?*'

I had with me John Stuart Mill's *Logic* and the *Oxford Book of Medieval Latin Verse*, and when we arrived at Spitzbergen the remoteness of my reading material chimed very nicely with that almost abstract landscape, a series of bold steep pyramids slashed out in black, white, and khaki. As for the only human beings on Spitzbergen, the unfortunate coal-miners (and the coal was low grade too), whose summer was a monotony of light, whose winter a monotony of night, whose only vegetation lichen, they struck me not as human beings but as walking, wild-eyed props. Perhaps most people then seemed props to me; I was still assimilating life

to the theatre, and the sort of plays I liked were *From Morn to Midnight* and *The Adding Machine*, both of which I had seen at the Oxford Playhouse.

My upbringing had made me very shy because so many human contacts in my father's Ulster parish were taboo. The Catholics were obviously taboo; most of the working classes were given to drink, bad language, and the throwing of rotten eggs; and many of the 'gentry' were ruled out because they were 'fast', which meant little more than that they kept a decanter of whiskey on the sideboard, gave bridge parties and dances, and went to race meetings. On the other hand the minority who were accepted by my family seemed to me on the whole, when they were not positively repellent, to be just plain boring. I was very snobbish about accents, and the Belfast accent struck me as not only the ugliest but the least aristocratic of the lot. All islands are insular but some seem more insular than others, and on my twenty-first birthday I was eaten up with envy of my friends who at that very moment were discovering Germany or Greece.

In 1928 it was a commonplace among undergraduates that Germany was 'the most civilized country in the world'. I often wonder what difference it would have made to me if I had had a Berlin to say goodbye to. But my knowledge of things German was, and has remained, second-hand. From the age of thirteen I had been addicted to the myths of the Northmen; my Valkyries being always ready to ride again, it seems strange that I missed Wagner. But at Oxford I did discover Nietzsche, beginning with *The Birth of Tragedy*, which I found a welcome, if perverse, antidote to the current brand of Philhellenism that so over-emphasized the reason. Next and inevitably, beguiled by the title, I plunged into *Thus Spake Zarathustra*, from which of course, given the slightest romantic leanings, anyone can extract almost anything he wants. At the same time I was flirting with Schopenhauer, being only too willing both to mimic his pessimism and to fumble through the dark night of the Will.

My philosophy tutor, one of Oxford's last neo-Hegelians, had encouraged me to look once—but only once—at the British empiricists and then to turn away to the German idealists, and, although I read these latter only in translation, their intervoluted jargon fell upon my ears (repeat 'ears') like an Open Sesame; the cave—excuse me, the club—was very select; the thieves—excuse me, the clubmen—had cornered the Absolute. While these predilections of mine presuppose both affectation and make-believe, I think they were also governed by something deeper. Having

[231]

been brought up in a traditionally religious family, and having, true to my period, reacted violently against the Christian dogma and, to some extent too, against the Christian ethic, I felt morally naked and spiritually hungry. So I was tempted to experiment simultaneously with two very different types of cure or defence—the Gallic grain of salt (recently, for instance, I had lapped up *Candide*) and the hidden magic of the Rheingold. Let everything either be vanity or One! It was to take me some time to close for a middle way.

When my undergraduate friends praised the 'civilization' of Germany they were not so much swayed by the above considerations as by the glamour of intellectual gatherings in Berlin and even more perhaps by the decadence of Berlin night-clubs. In the former, it seemed, politics, which in Oxford were still unfashionable, had blossomed out into a dashing form of Communism much less fusty than anything to be found in Britain or Russia—though I *had* been attracted by what I had heard of Soviet experiments in non-naturalistic theatre and naturalistic divorce. As for Decadence, any form of this was an assertion of the rights of man. Oxford was then in transition, most of the Ambrose Silks and other Evelyn Waugh veterans having gone down.

At the first Oxford party I was taken to as a freshman, in October 1927, the only drink was champagne in tumblers, and there was a beautiful young man who spent the whole evening in the same armchair, talking to no one except a stuffed spotted dog which he joggled up and down on its lead. But there were few more parties of this sort, and, though one or two male undergraduates still used powder and lipstick, and to get on in the O.U.D.S. it still helped if one were or pretended to be homosexual (a fact which prevented me joining the O.U.D.S.), the Oxford Decadence was all but over, and anyhow, I thought, could not even at its peak or nadir have competed with these mysterious goings-on in Berlin. We were nearly all of us ashamed, at least as regards culture, of being British; almost anything from the Continent, including its vice, was assumed to be more 'significant' than its British counterpart. I was therefore delighted when in 1928 I met my first German baron.

This baron had a sallow complexion, long black fingernails, and an insidious bonhomie. 'Soon,' he would say, 'we must have a jolly Bierabend.' I think he may have come to my rooms for the first time when I was giving tea to Walter de la Mare, who was visiting Oxford to lecture on poetry. I took to de la Mare very much as a person, but had little

interest in his forthcoming lecture because he was not 'avant-garde'. The baron on the other hand was assumed to be very avant-garde. He let us know that he was surf-riding on the crest of a wonderful new movement, of which I had not heard, called Nazi; this apparently enabled him to offer us free trips to Germany by air. Soon after our first meeting he revealed that he was a journalist and showed me an article in a German newspaper in which my rooms in Merton were described as though I were the Rimbaud of my day, making original movements with my hands among candles stuck in bottles and original modern paintings (in reality Zwemmer prints).

I asked the baron to lunch, carefully providing hock. Two of my other guests were Jewesses, whom I regarded as highly cosmopolitan; I was much disappointed by their reaction to the baron. Next the baron went visiting Eton for his paper, and his enthusiasm for English poetry grew till he started reciting, in a guttural 'poetry voice' and with a lush over-emphasis, 'When the hounds of Spring are on Winter's traces'. Swinburne being despised in our circles, I began to think the baron was not so avant-garde after all. Very soon he was boring me so much that I used to dodge him in the street. Then someone discovered that he was only an adoptive baron. Which explained his dirty fingernails, and that, of course, was that.

As the baron faded out, my Jewish friends (one of whom I afterwards married) came up into the foreground with a flash of primary colours and a strong waft of chypre. I had never known any Jews, and now found that, in addition to the guilt of insularity, I ought to be ashamed of being Gentile. It was transpiring that Jews were in every way far more sensitive than other people, being all of them like the princess on the nine mattresses. Sometimes I had doubts about this, e.g. when Christianity was disposed of by the rhetorical question 'How can three people be one person?' but what did strike me in the face was a superabundant vitality. How pale, I thought, in comparison are the Ulster curates, the Old Marlburians, the tired dons, and the bored housewives.

Also, these people had travelled, and their memories seemed stocked from the Arabian Nights: there were relatives in India, jewel merchants, whose daughters spent their days on silken cushions measuring each other's eyelashes and running the rubies through their fingers; and there had been a pigeon fancier in Bagdad; and balls in Bucharest; and so on and so on, all glitter and bubble and fanfare. To me this seemed, though later I found I was mistaken, to be the very opposite of puritanism and a marvellous escape from petit bourgeois mentality.

But, even while I was succumbing to these Scheherazades, I was still keeping up with (or down? down on the earth with) the Joneses. At one of the very few lecture courses I attended at all regularly I was irritated by the faces of two most intense young men who were said to be sure of their Firsts. If people who look so boring can get Firsts, I thought, I must get one too—only I will do it more gracefully; I will lounge my way in like Petronius Arbiter. The names of my two irritants, I discovered, were Quintin McGarel Hogg and R. H. S. Crossman.

Which brings me back to politics and to what later was called social consciousness. Auden and Spender were at Oxford at the time, but their poetry had barely become political. Auden already indeed thought of modern society as diseased, and was stressing the 'clinical' approach; flowers and such things were vulgar or trivial and the proper study of the modern poet was man, man being the congeries of a lot of pretty nasty *specimens*. But the specimens *could* get out of the killing-bottle (soon the escape was to be Marx-cum-Freud, then—much later—the Anglo-Catholic Church) if they took a tip from D. H. Lawrence; it was thanks to Auden that I first read Lawrence and added *The White Peacock* and *Twilight in Italy* to my short list of sacred books.

It may be that Auden was already becoming Teutonically left-wing, and he had after all driven a vehicle for the strikers during the General Strike, but I cannot remember him at that time doing any political propaganda; his gospel seemed to be much more the Lawrentian one of spiritual revival through instinct but qualified by the cerebral methods of the 'clinic'. The only undergraduate poet who seemed thoroughly committed to Socialism was Clere Parsons, who died soon after he left Oxford. Yet Parsons's poetry, far from being political propaganda, consisted of experimental lyrics in the manner of E. E. Cummings, while as a person— and here he prefigured the ' 'Thirties Poets'—he did not look at all like a man who was at home with the masses. The Decadents had at least been self-consistent; their successors were to find themselves tugged at by incompatibles, feeling things they had renounced and professing beliefs they hardly felt.

Take, for instance, the question of class. There were many undergraduates like myself who theoretically conceded that all men were equal, but who, in practice, while only too willing to converse, or attempt to, with say Normandy peasants or shopkeepers, would wince away in their own college halls from those old grammar school boys who with impure

[234]

vowels kept admiring Bernard Shaw or Noël Coward while grabbing their knives and forks like dumb-bells. Thus I was horrified one day to receive a letter from some Poor Relations—a middle-aged and, I suspected, ungrammatical couple—suggesting they should come to tea with me. Then I remembered I had an 'oak'. As soon as the dreaded visitors had been corralled in my rooms in college I explained to them the old Oxford custom of the two doors in the one doorway: once the outer one, the oak, had been 'sported', no one could get in from outside. 'The idea,' I said, 'is to leave one undisturbed to work.' 'Look!' I said, sporting it quickly and forgetting to open it again. The idea was to protect my snobbery from callers; and so it did, but the bad taste still recurs to me. This fear of being caught with the wrong people was constant, and the world seemed full of wrong people. Americans, however uncouth, were different; I knew a number of Rhodes Scholars who, however they dressed or spoke, could always be explained away as either exotic or comic. And all college servants, of course, were comic and usually 'period' too, straight out of Rowlandson or Cruikshank, collectors' pieces and talking points. In fact in the social game the more hayseed one's American friend, or the more illiterate one's scout, the better. Like illustrations to *Punch* they were props rather than people.

Still, people in general were a perpetual menace. At school several of us who belonged to the intellectual minority had developed elaborate and sometimes paradoxical defence mechanisms. My own was to stick my neck out. Although I disliked being stared at, when I first went up to Oxford I made a point of dressing eccentrically, growing long side-whiskers and pitching my voice up whenever my opinions were un-popular. When I got an angry reaction, such as someone calling after me in the street 'Is your name Daphne with the long hair!' I felt I had scored, even though I was embarrassed.

The absurd old Oxford antithesis of Aesthete and Hearty was still going strong. It was not only a point of honour to show which side one belonged to; it also, even at the risk of violence to one's clothes, person, or property, gave a peculiar sense of security. By my twenty-first birthday, however, I no longer felt so partisan, and I was annoyed in the following term when a very affected freshman (described by Father Knox as looking like one of those insipid old-fashioned dolls which close their eyes when you lay them on their sides) pulled out a lavatory chain, while walking with me in the Turl, and hit a large hearty across the face with it.

I was beginning to feel that provocation of people was wasteful. But this did not mean that I was drawing nearer to people. In my last year at school, when I was sharing a study with Anthony Blunt, whose chief interest was already in the visual arts although he was specializing still in mathematics, I had agreed with him that People were of minor importance compared with Things. Whether I had ever completely believed this or not, I still certainly thought that a good many things were preferable to a good many people. This is perhaps why I so much enjoyed both *Ulysses* and *Mrs Dalloway*. Both Poldy Bloom and Mrs Dalloway are not so much active characters as people possessed by the things that have crammed their memories and the things that impinge on their senses. If I had only come across Rilke then, this further levitation of Things would have certainly made me canonize him. As it was, I spent much of my time at Oxford alone, staring at cylinders of brawn in the grocer's or at the sluices in Mesopotamia, comparing the visual aspects of things and standing Plato on his head to insist that Appearance was more real than what he would have called Reality.

That I had to make comparisons, to find that x looks like y, was of course a drawback; but then I was not a painter, though I often wished I was. At the age of seventeen I had swallowed Clive Bell's doctrine of Significant Form; at eighteen I had repudiated this, but at nineteen, on my first visit to Paris, I had found myself saying of a bridge across the Seine 'How significant that is!', to which my companion, being an incipient philosopher, replied 'Significant of what?' At twenty-one I still thought that the look of things—or sometimes the sound or the smell or the feel of them—could be more important than the things themselves, whatever *they* might be (though, as compared with 'people', I often tended to equate these sensible aspects of the thing with the thing itself; hence my acceptance of Blunt's schoolboy dictum). By now I had also discovered (long before Mr Aldous Huxley played about with mescalin) what an ally alcohol was in these matters.

When I was drunk, I found, things could either look more so, themselves with an added emphasis, or swoop off into fantasy and look like quite other things; in either case the change seemed an improvement. I also noticed that, on a morning after, something very simple, like an earthenware pot of flowers or the clock across the quad or an earthenware pot empty, could fill my whole consciousness like a solid meal—or was this perhaps going for a ride on a tiger, was the thing

perceived making a meal of *me*? So, though I had not yet read Rimbaud, I began to experiment in a certain *dérèglement des sens*. Not, of course, that this was my only reason for getting drunk; it was also obviously a challenge to convention and a quick way out of the Valley of Diffidence. During this year I was to get arrested for drunkenness and spend a defiant hour or two singing in my cell to a tune of Schubert's 'That was in another country and besides the wench is dead'. I had not had any wench by that date.

In my twenty-second year, then, the sheer look of things probably exercised me more than it ever has since. It was also the heyday of my bookishness; books were tokens, talismans, keys to a lost kingdom. Again, of course, there was snobbery involved; just as mantelpieces had been made to prove one was invited out, bookshelves were there to show one was really *in*. While one *had* to admire *The Waste Land*, one *could* not have been seen reading Galsworthy. In fact *The Waste Land* did appeal to me; I understood it much better than I did *Prufrock*, for instance, in which I completely missed the humour, as I did in much of *Ulysses*. This surely is understandable. However deep one's ignorance, historically, of the Decline of the West, it has been since World War I something that must hit one in the marrow at adolescence; anyhow Waste Lands are not only community phenomena, there must be one somewhere in each individual just as everyone contains in himself those places which Spenser described as the Cave of Despair, the House of Busyrane, and, thank God, the Garden of Adonis.

The Waste Land, therefore, hit me in the way a person hits one. But the bulk of my reading was not on this thou-thou plane; many books I went to not as ends but as means in a Robinson Crusoe effort to knock up my own *Weltanschauung* (I would certainly, not only for reasons of snobbery but of magic, have preferred the German word to its English equivalent). Some of these books were my prescribed texts for Greats, and among these, oddly it might seem, in view of my romantic disposition, I was beginning to prefer Aristotle to Plato. Which is perhaps not so odd after all. It was Shelley, the most Platonizing of our poets, who wrote:

> Life, like a dome of many-coloured glass,
> Stains the white radiance of Eternity,

whereas people like myself must always prefer the Twopence Coloured to even the Pound Plain. For all his famous dryness, Aristotle, being among

[237]

other things a zoologist, never let transcendental radiance destroy the shapes of the creatures or impose a white-out on everything.

This is probably why I was so fascinated not only by D. H. Lawrence but by *The Dance of Life* by Havelock Ellis, a book which I have not read for thirty years and which now might very well bore me. What I hankered for was unity in difference, and Ellis's not original concept of all life as a dance was so fully illustrated in the concrete and over such a wide range, from the courting ritual of birds to the virtues of aberrant spelling, that I thought 'Now I'm really getting hot!' But at the same time I found an equal, and more fashionable, satisfaction in the polemical writings of Wyndham Lewis, even though often he was attacking some of my own favourites; for instance he attacked the 'child cult' for which I had a strong weakness—but here once more, no doubt, I wanted to have my cake and eat it. The two main things that appealed to me in Lewis were his destructive criticism and his constructive demands for system and firm outlines; these two came together in his eulogies of works like *Timon of Athens*. I had at the time—and here my own age (for twenty-year-olds have always been seduced by Hamlet) clicked with the period I was living in—a preference for Shakespeare at his most sombre and apparently destructive. I had already grown tired of pinprick satire, and had no wish to read *Point Counter Point* when it came out in 1928, but despair and disgust in the grand manner enlivened me. I found Donne's Sermons and Jeremy Taylor's *Holy Dying* excellent for reading aloud, and one of my favourite Shakespeare characters was Thersites. But I was also very fond of Tchehov's short stories.

So there I was, caught between bonfires and backfires, like many of my contemporaries. Much self-deception lay ahead of me. Not long after my twenty-first birthday I became engaged to be married, which very much altered my day-to-day life in Oxford. I had less time for reading or talking with my friends and was encouraged instead to listen to gramophone records of Sophie Tucker the Red-Hot Momma and Jack Smith the Whispering Baritone. I even learned to foxtrot, but never, though this was its period, to charleston. And I tried to cultivate optimism and a belief in the domestic virtues.

In the summer of 1929 I spent four weeks in the island of Achill and six weeks at St Tropez. The former place was inhabited by stage patriarchs on stage donkeys, the latter by stage Frenchmen who lolled on a stage beach. People were not only a menace, they were also something of an

illusion; of course in Ireland, my own country, I now felt hopelessly anglicized, and, as for Frenchmen, I could not follow what they said. In both the West of Ireland and in France my books of philosophy seemed more out of place than they had the year before in the Arctic Circle. My tutor had been a pupil of F. H. Bradley, and I was very fond of Bradley's dictum that every judgment (in the logical sense of the word) is a judgment about the universe. It was exciting, when I said I liked aubergine, to be saying something true about the universe—and moreover to be adding something to it; still, it did not help me to understand the Provençal woman who had cooked the aubergine and who after all was in the universe too.

When I returned to Oxford for my fourth year, many of my exact contemporaries had gone down at the end of their third and some had already got jobs. Their letters had a whiff of what reluctantly I granted were wider spheres; people in Oxford seemed to know all the questions, but earning a weekly wage was at least one answer to something. Some of my friends who had no ideas about careers used to turn to Father D'Arcy, who was said to have much influence with concerns like I.C.I. Though I admired Father D'Arcy, expert on Aquinas and master carver of game, as a man who had both feet in both worlds, he too, like more secular Oxford intellectuals, seemed to bear the stamp of the Hothouse (a cliché still used today by Oxford undergraduates of their alma mater).

Anyhow, I joined neither I.C.I. nor the Church of Rome, but got married and went to live in Birmingham, thus exchanging, at first, a public hothouse for a private one. But, as the panes of glass fell gradually out of their frames, while the plants inside were endangered, I began to smell the life that went on outside and to notice—but only gradually— that what had seemed walking props were really persons like myself. All that, though, was still in the future. I was still *in statu pupillari*, working for an archaic examination and given to quoting from a poem in Ezra Pound's *Cathay* (about a middle-aged Chinese who had failed in *his* examinations): 'But all this comes to an end and is not again to be met with.' All this did. And it was high time.

[239]

RETROSPECTION

We had planned to celebrate our coming-of-age with the compilation of an impressive Index of all our distinguished contributors and the manifold subjects upon which they have so delightfully informed us through the years. Then the suspicion entered our mind that perhaps we were beginning to take ourselves too seriously, as has happened even with the creators of such frivolities as the *Pink 'Un* or *Esquire*. (There's a thought for our old age: the writing of a book of wistful reminiscences with the title *Old Saturday Book Days!*) So, instead, we have assembled a random alphabetical sequence of topics that have been touched upon and have picked out a few of our favourite pictures to illustrate them. If any fourth-year student wants to write a thesis upon Saturday Attitudes here are his references. (The numbers in brackets are the numbers of the volumes referred to.)

RCHITECTURE has yielded Saturdiurnal essays as profound and various as Sir Julian Huxley's on Petra (9) Lady Kelly's on Persepolis (17) and Russia (14), John Betjeman's on Sir Ninian Comper, railway stations, and garden cities (18), and Robert Harling's, in this issue, on Le Corbusier, Mies van der Rohe, *et al*. The architectural feature we liked as much as any, however, was Vivien Greene's on dolls' and baby houses (17), of which you see one of Edwin Smith's photographs above.

ALLET, we must admit, had so splendid a run in our pages in the days of The Founder, that we have not dared to return to it since. The photograph above, of Tamara Toumanova and George Skibine dancing a *pas de deux* from *Don Quixote*, is from a wonderful series by Howard Byrne (10).

UTTERFLIES have fluttered from time to time over the Saturday *salmagundi* prepared by Olive Cook and Edwin Smith. But in Number Nineteen, inspired by Sir Winston Churchill's entomological enthusiasm, L. Hugh Newman gave us an enchanting piece on butterflies as garden pets rather than specimens on pins. The peacock plate above came from Benjamin Wilkes's great eighteenth-century monograph on the subject.

LOTHES—or the lack of them—have inspired some of
our favourite Saturday correspondents, such as the late
lamented Willett Cunnington (15 and 16) and the yet
present James Laver, to whose essay on artists' models (15)
the Renoir painting above was an illustration. The lady on
the opposite page did not appear as a 'model', in any sense; but she takes
her due alphabetical place here as one of the illustrations to Raymond
Mortimer's delightful piece in Number 15 on CROQUET.

AMEOS and CONVERSATION PIECES—both
may be taken as visual and literal expressions of the Saturday
spirit. The cameos so exquisitely photographed by Edwin
Smith on the opposite page (9) came from the storehouse of
that visionary jeweller, the late Moysheh Oyved, and reflect
in onyx, agate, coral, and opal the enthusiasm of the eighteenth-century
dilettante for classical themes. The eighteenth century is also reflected,
vividly and with no less artifice, in the portrait group of the Rookes
Leeds family above, which is perhaps the masterpiece of that master of
the conversation piece, Arthur Devis. Sacheverell Sitwell wrote about
Devis and his work in Number 12, and we ourselves have turned back
again and again to the refreshment offered by such elegance and self-
composure, caught in a moment of time and a shimmer of silks and satin.

CATS will continue to be favoured Saturday subjects as long as the present felinophile Editor holds his job. Some colour drawings of cats, in human contexts, by Archie Mason in Number 18, were immensely popular. The two Siamese were photographed by Dunscombe Honiball (9).

OGS—dare we hazard the proposition?—are not *quite* so 'Saturday' as cats. By which statement all we mean is that many thousands of admirable and dedicated dog-lovers are not what we would regard as characteristic S.B. readers. Still, our Founder had his beloved and unique Coco. And we have always loyally tried to give dogs their due in our pages—as witness this photograph in Number 16 by Kathleen Eachus.

EMBROIDERY is not, in general, a male pursuit. We are surprised, therefore, to observe how often the art of needlework has been written about and illustrated in our man-edited pages. Perhaps the influence of our constant contributor, Olive Cook, is to be detected here. Certainly it was she who thought to illustrate a study of Christmas in Number 13 with the fourteenth-century embroidered Nativity shown on the opposite page.

FLOWERS, in one guise or another, have adorned each of our twenty-one numbers. H. E. Bates wrote about sea flowers on the first page of our first number. Viscount Kemsley's superb copy of *The Temple of Flora* yielded a series of colour plates in Number 8. And Wilfrid Blunt wrote a masterly essay on Dutch 'primitives' of flower painting in Number 17. We still await the crowning recognition of our labours, however: the exhibition at the Chelsea Flower Show of a new rose (or iris, or lily) named 'Saturday Book'.

LASS is a pre-eminently Saturdiurnal substance. The words 'looking glass' have appeared in our sub-titles on many occasions, and the translucent properties of 'lead crystal' have often attracted the eye and lens of Edwin Smith. In the decoration of glass, moreover, the S.B. can claim to have made a positive contribution to contemporary arts and crafts, in that we were the first organ to publish a full appraisal of the diamond-point engravings on glass by Laurence Whistler (in Number 10). At the same time The Founder acquired from Mr Whistler a set of six glasses, engraved with insect designs, which were subsequently exhibited in the Festival of Britain. The Stonehenge glass shown above was illustrated in a second appraisal of Laurence Whistler's work in Number 16. We take some pride in having introduced to the world at large a craftsman of unique accomplishment, much of whose work has been executed for readers of *The Saturday Book*.

HATS are the expression of personality, of whim, of gaiety and *joie de vivre*. They are permissibly odd, absurd, eccentric, and dotty—but always, of course, delightful. All of which might be said, we hope, of *The Saturday Book* itself. The hats that have appeared in our pages—especially Mary Eden's feature in Number 17—would adorn a full-scale Easter Parade.

ORSES have trotted, cantered, and even galloped (like Toulouse-Lautrec's, above) through our pages, despite the fact that both The Founder and his successor have better seats in the editorial chair than in the saddle. The Horse, however, is much more than a means of locomotion: it is a social symbol and an aesthetic inspiration. We love Society and dote on Art.

H A W K S—fierce, cruel, predatory creatures—would hardly seem to be at home among our Elian pages. Yet aesthetically they are akin to the horse. What a superb visual complement is Gould's Kite to Toulouse-Lautrec's racehorse. And what a glittering piece on hawks Kenneth Allsop contributed (19).

*I*NVENTIONS of consequence, such as the H-bomb and the turbo-jet, mean extremely little to the present Editor, or, indeed, The Founder. Both of us, however, have a weakness for inventions of what might be called Currier & Ives vintage, such as the first film projector, shown below, which was patented in 1897 and was used in combination with the Magic Lantern. In our time we have also celebrated the Shaving Engine (13), the Aerial Steam Carriage and the Umbrello Machine (14), and a variety of Mechanical Musicians (15).

*J*EWELS, lovely 'jools'; a quintessential Saturday subject: the colour, the sparkle, the intricacies of craftsmanship and design, not to mention the connotations of love, romance, wealth, and avarice. And yet, curiously enough, it is almost impossible to do justice to the beauty of jewels in colour illustration. Now and again Edwin Smith has hit it off; but he has found that the lens of his camera can create a new and uncommon beauty out of the forms and lights and shadows of jewelry in simple black-and-white. As you look at the photograph opposite, do you not agree?

NICK-KNACKS—that is how a cruel critic once stigmatized the subject-matter of our pages. Quite right, too. We are content to leave the discussion of higher-level themes to Sir K. Clark, Sir H. Read, Sir C. Snow, and other knightly taste-shapers, let alone the Hipsters and the Zen Buddhists. We are perfectly happy gazing at the frivolous gee-gaws above.

LOVE, of course, is a more serious matter, and we wouldn't dare to take it lightly. In our time we have studied in our pages some very serious lovers, such as Don Juan (3), Skittles and Mrs Gladstone (8), Ethel M. Dell (15), and the Rosetti-Morris Triangle (18). In Number 10 Ronald Searle anatomized Love with his aseptic pen. One of our favourite contributions on this theme, however, was the series of early Staffordshire courtship groups in the Fitzwilliam Museum, which were reproduced in Number 16. The one above is charmingly entitled 'Perswaition'.

USIC, may be, is one of our blind spots, despite the fact that in Number Four the Founder announced the engagement of the London Philharmonic Orchestra to give a Saturday Book Concert at the Albert Hall. The present Editor, though a hero-worshipper of Yehudi Menuhin and the Amadeus String Quartet, has never organized a concert, and takes the view, rightly or wrongly, that musical criticism is Sunday rather than

Saturday material. Still, he did publish in Number 15 a masterly research into Mechanical Musicians, by Jeremy Sandford. Marianne Droz, opposite, is one of them. (She is worked by a barrel with pins, which operates levers going through her elbows to her fingers.) We have also done our duty by Jazz: as witness the present Number, and an ex-cathedra utterance by Humphrey Lyttelton in the first Number we edited (12). We can therefore index our musical activities appropriately—and alphabetically—with the above photograph of MORTON, JELLY ROLL.

NUDES, when painted by Velazquez, above, or Ingres, below, call for no justification. The year after these paintings appeared in our pages (15), however, we heard that an old lady in Lichfield had told her bookseller to cancel her order. 'Never mind,' said our Publisher stoically, 'I daresay two old gentlemen in Leicester increased theirs.'

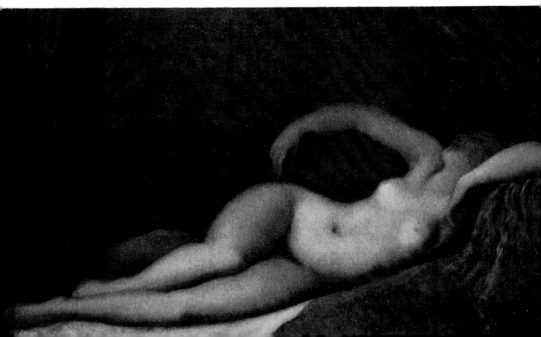

LIVIER is perhaps a refutation of the theory that *The Saturday Book* is not concerned with greatness. Dilys Powell surveyed his early career in Number 6, and he himself contributed a piece on the actor's craft in Number 5. The portrait by Dali appeared in Number 20. Yes, Olivier has greatness. But his performance as Archie Rice had a certain 'Saturday' flavour, too.

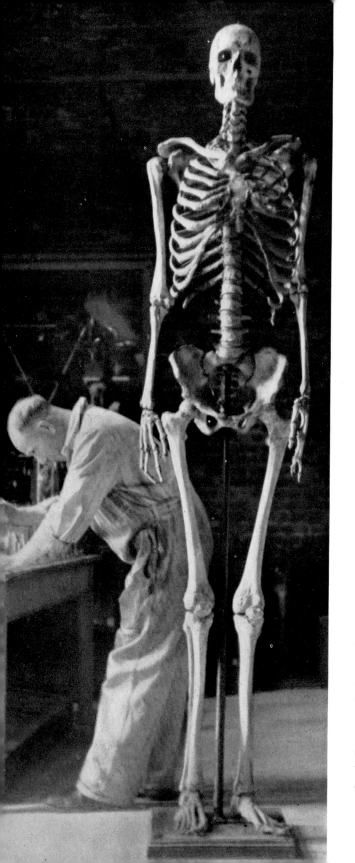

EOPLE are the stuff and substance of the *Saturday* formula (if there is such a thing). The present Editor, therefore, was slightly chagrined when the *Times Lit. Supp.*, reviewing the first Number under his editorship, said that whereas his predecessor was interested in people, he was obviously more interested in *things*. The comment was probably fair: that's why it has stuck in our mind all these years. But we have, we hope, gone quite a way, since then, to humanize our pages. Admittedly, the kinds of people we are interested in tend to be off-beat. We haven't given a fair showing (indeed, any showing at all) to politicians, generals, Trade Union leaders or American Presidents. We believe S.B. readers turn to our pages for insight into less conventional figures, such as the Moat Farm Murderer, whose 'confession' appeared in Number 1, or Eli Culbertson (Bertrand Russell wrote about him in Number 10), or May Tofts, who 'bred' rabbits (11), 'Monk' Lewis, Dr Graham of the Temple of Health (16), Gertrude Jekyll (16), Alexis Soyer (18), or Frank Harris (19). And nobody, of course, could apply the word 'conventional' to our perennial diarist, Fred Bason.

[264]

RINCESSES, fairy or actual, are the one element in the Establishment which we regard as 100 per cent 'Saturday'. Royalist to the core, and romantic to a fault, we dote on them. And there's no picture we have put into our pages which continues to thrill us more than this painting in the Royal Collection at Windsor, by an unknown artist, of Elizabeth the First when she was thirteen years old and as yet unburdened by the crown.

QUEEN ELIZABETH THE FIRST has not been the subject of a special S.B. feature, but we included the famous Rainbow Portrait from Hatfield House (below) in our twelfth Number, never realizing that one day we should reprint it opposite the portrait of the same sitter at the age of thirteen. 'Look here, upon this picture, and on this.'

NON SINE SOLE
IRIS.

RIDING, as we mentioned earlier, is not an outstanding accomplishment of The Founder or of the present Editor. Yet the Horse recurs, again and again, in our pages, even in such odd guises as the Staffordshire salt-glaze figure above, the Astbury-Whieldon musketeer's mount on the left, or the statue on the Capitol steps opposite. Clearly there must be a psychological explanation for this. Clowns long to play Hamlet; Prime Ministers yearn to keep pigs; and doubtless we hackney writers, clip-clopping over the cobbles in the narrow lanes off Grub-street, have some thwarted ambition to be galloping across a stiff line of country somewhere in the shires, on a tearing scent, taking yawners and five-barred gates in our stride.

ROME seems to have usurped the position traditionally held by Paris as the cynosure of gilded gaiety. *La vie Parisienne* has become *la dolce vita*. Whilst nothing, ever, will dislodge us from our loyalty to the Place Vendôme and Saint-Germain-des-Prés, we must admit that *Saturdiurnalia* have something in common with Saturnalia. Above is one of a fine series of Roman views by Peter and Roderick Pryor (12).

ROSA MUSCOSA
Edwards

ROSA MUSCOSA VARIGATA
Andrews

ROSA SULPHUREA AILSON
Edwards

ROSA SEMPER FLORENS
Andrews

ROSES, it seems, are Saturday's flowers. Olive Cook plucked some superb blooms, including a folding colour plate of a Fantin Latour, for Number 11. Some of her bouquet are to be seen on the opposite page. Yet, though we yield to none in our love of the Queen of Flowers, we have indulged at times in other green thoughts. In Number 17 we printed a most erudite study by Wilfrid Blunt of the primitive Flemish flower painters, and in the same issue John Nash wrote an enchanting piece on vintage window plants.

SEASIDE: we do like to be beside it. Edwin Smith and Olive Cook like to, too. Indeed, the Seaside has inspired them to some of their most piquant discoveries. The Polka title on the right and the Swansea porcelain plate below are happy examples.

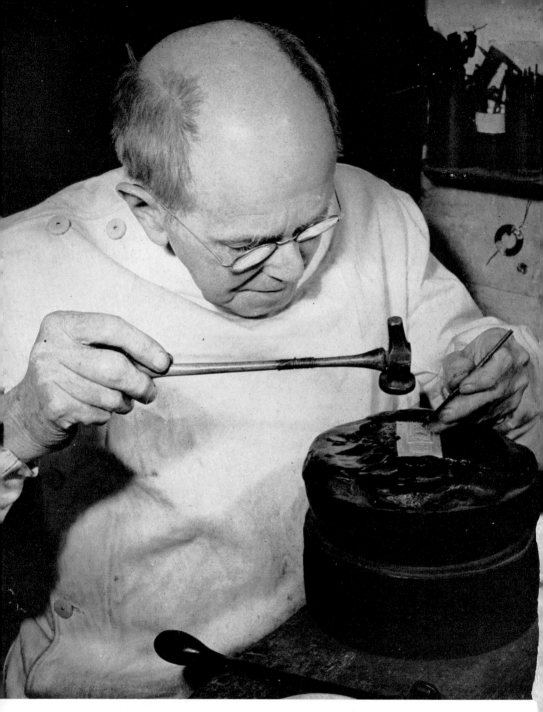

ILVER is, of all tactile materials used for works of art, one of the most photogenic. And the photographs of Silver which have been reproduced in *The Saturday Book* give us a purer aesthetic pleasure than almost anything else—even than Edwin Smith's fine photographs, in Number 9, of Benvenuto Cellini's famous golden salt-cellar from Vienna. The Warwick silver cruet illustrated here was made in 1746 by Samuel Wood. This superb photograph is one of a series taken by Raymond Fortt for the S.B. to illustrate an appreciation of antique English silver by Jonathan Stone in Number 19. The photograph of the modern silversmith opposite—if so venerable and traditional a figure can be called modern—was one of a series illustrating craftsmen at work taken by Tom Jones for Number 16.

TAINED GLASS. What drama, what tenseness of human emotion, is revealed in these details from the Miracles of St Thomas in Canterbury Cathedral, which were among the fine series of photographs by Birkin Haward illustrating a study by Norman Scarfe in Number 18.

SATURDAY PAINTING is a term invented by the Editor and Olive Cook (so we claim), in Number 19, to distinguish the amateur painting of people distinguished professionally in other spheres from the Sunday painting produced by untrained unsophisticates. The signature reveals the artist of the Jamaican scene above. The painting below is by Spike Milligan; the title is 'When Did You Last See Your Father?'

EA AND TOXOPHILY have little in common except their initial letter and the fact that both have yielded delightful and informative features in our pages. The photograph above is by Reece Winston, one of our favourite photographers, who provided a vivid series of pictures of trade signs in Number 14. Tea-addicts should also make a note of Griselda Lewis's survey of teapots in Number 15. It was in this issue, too, that Victor Mitzakis's photographic studies of the Royal Toxophilites appeared —the archer opposite is Mrs Flower, Lady Champion of England.

T RAINS: we were always addicted to trains (see page 288), and if we'd room we would index this subject with Frith's 'Railway Station', which we reproduced as a folding plate in Number 10—a painting we like even more than 'Derby Day'. As it is, we must content ourselves with the silk picture above, which represents the first train, built by George Stephenson in 1825, and another silk picture (below), woven by Thomas Stevens and depicting 'The Present Time', when 'Lord Howe' was capable of travelling at the terrifying speed of sixty miles an hour.

The S.B. can claim to have taken its part in the inculcation of a proper respect for the Railway Age. Readers will remember last year's masterly photographs of the Talyllyn Railway by Edwin Smith, with commentary by that railway enthusiast, L. T. C. Rolt. This prompts us to pay our editorial tribute to this remarkable, right-thinking, erudite historian of industrial art, who has contributed valuable pieces on veteran and vintage cars (Number 13: long before *Genevieve*), on traction engines (15), and on mines and tunnels (14).

Oh yes, the locomotive opposite, leaving sharp on 12.43, was painted by the Belgian surrealist, Rene Magritte, on whose precise and delicate art we had a piece in Number 19.

UNCANNY STORIES are traditionally a constituent of all annuals. Perhaps we have not included as many as we might, but as that unexpected person, L. T. C. Rolt (see under *Trains*), pointed out in a study of the Ghost Story in Number 16, ghosts are not what they were. We did have the honour, however, of printing what we believe to be the spookiest poem written by John Betjeman (16), and we shall never forget the feeling of mounting horror as we first read Walter de la Mare's 'An Anniversary' (12). This was not strictly a ghost story, but its uncanniness was almost intolerable. We doubt very much whether the ethereal lady above (17) is either a ghost or uncanny. We suspect the presence of suspensory apparatus. But we applaud her unknown photographer— circa 1900, we surmise.

ENICE—oh yes, we fall every time for that aged Siren of the Adriatic, *despite* the tourists and the pigeons milling round the Campanile. But we admit we *were* rather relieved, and excited, when Barbara Gomperts brought in the series of Venetian views we printed in Number 19: one of them is seen above. Show us better and less hackneyed photographs of Venice, if you can.

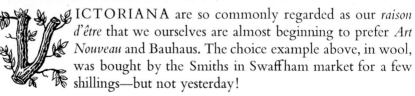 ICTORIANA are so commonly regarded as our *raison d'être* that we ourselves are almost beginning to prefer *Art Nouveau* and Bauhaus. The choice example above, in wool, was bought by the Smiths in Swaffham market for a few shillings—but not yesterday!

ALKING, when we first reproduced (11) this print of Captain Barclay walking a thousand miles in a thousand successive hours in 1809, was rather looked down upon as the recreation of the vulgar. Not today! Does Dr Barbara Moore, perhaps, read *The Saturday Book*?

is a letter which usually baffles Alphabetists. Not us, however. We could give you Xerxes, of whose full-length portrait in bas-relief, at Persepolis, we printed a fine colour photograph by Lady Kelly in Number 17. But instead we are giving you XYLOGRAPHY, which, as you doubtless know, means the art of engraving on wood—an art which has been fostered by Founder and Editor since the first S.B. appeared with lovely wood-engraved decorations by Agnes Miller Parker. The engraving above is by Robert Giblings, another master of the craft, who wrote and engraved delightfully for us in Numbers 10, 12, 14, 16, and 17.

YACHTS: 'A' Class Raters on the Thames at Bourne End. And as 'Saturday' a picture as most of our readers could wish for. Curiously, it wasn't until Number 17 that we got round to small boats, as distinct from sailing vessels of the past (10) and the *Titanic* (12). When we did we had the good luck to get a sunlit and windswept bunch of photographs from Eileen Ramsey, who is extraordinarily adroit at capturing in her lens the beauty of sail.

ZINCOGRAPHY. It could equally well, in view of our choice of illustrations, be ZOOLOGY. But these two sets of four-colour halftone process blocks happen to be rather good examples of the art and craft of etching on zinc (or copper), which is what Zincography means. And this is the opportunity for us to pay tribute to the artists and craftsmen who, more than anyone else, are responsible for the success of *The Saturday Book*. From the beginning the great majority of our blocks have been made by an old-established firm, the Grout Engraving Company. To their tradition of craftsmanship, and to the skill and judgment of their individual craftsmen, the book owes much. In thanking them for all they have done anonymously and in conscientious pursuit of their craft we would like to mention by name their chief, Mr Kew, who has always taken a personal pride in *The Saturday Book*, and Mr Pat O'Sullivan, who has steered the course of our illustrations from film transparency to copper and zinc with unfailing care, speed, and good humour. To our printers, too, we express our indebtedness: first to Mr William Fisher and Mr John Gordon, of Fisher Knight & Company, and latterly to Mr Willis and his colleagues at the Anchor Press. Not the least of the pleasures of editorship is the happiness of working with friendly, helpful, sensitive people in a trade that preserves its traditional standards and its pride in its work.

POSTCRIPT. The Publishers, with that passion for publicity which has consumed them since the days of the unspeakable Curll (They wouldn't be publishers, though, would they, if they didn't believe in publicity?) have suggested that this Coming-of-age Number ought to contain a photograph of the present Editor. Well, here it is: taken some hundreds of years ago, in Saturday mood, it seems, though obviously in Sunday suit. The locomotive, even then, was evidently a 'vintage' one.

The initial letters in the foregoing pages were specially drawn for THE SATURDAY BOOK *by William McLaren.*

[288]